W9-BNH-168

ALL *Cakes* CONSIDERED

ALL *Cakes* CONSIDERED

A YEAR'S WORTH OF WEEKLY RECIPES TESTED, TASTED, AND APPROVED BY THE STAFF OF NPR'S *ALL THINGS CONSIDERED*

by Melissa Gray

Photographs by Annabelle Breakey and Stephen Voss

CHRONICLE BOOKS
SAN FRANCISCO

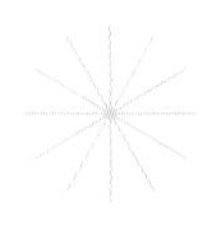

Dedicated to my Momma, **FAYE GUNN GRAY**

The first person I ever baked with and still my favorite person to bake with

Library of Congress Cataloging-in-Publication Data available.

ISBN 978-0-8118-6781-8

Manufactured in China

Designed by Leone Design, Tony Leone with layout assistance by Jon Akland

Food styling by Robyn Valarik
Prop styling by Alessandra Mortola

10 9 8 7 6 5 4 3 2 1

Chronicle Books LLC
680 Second Street
San Francisco, California 94107

www.chroniclebooks.com

CONTENTS

FOREWORD

Melissa Gray is one of those talented people whose voices are never heard, but whose work behind the scenes gets *All Things Considered* on the radio every weekday. As a producer on the NPR afternoon news magazine, she is part of a team that strives to make the day's events and other interesting developments both intelligible and listenable for two hours, Monday through Friday. Several million Americans drive home better informed, and possibly smiling, thanks to the show we call *ATC*. As a host of that show, as one whose voice is heard, I knowingly benefit directly from her newsy smarts and Southern wit; if you are a listener, then you benefit as well, and now you know it.

Melissa's many gifts include a taste for baking (which is the subject of this book), an ear for radio, and a profound sense of irony. Two examples of that last gift are (1) she prepared for an utterly nonvisual career, producing radio, by going to art school and (2) she asked me to write the foreword to this magisterial work on baking for the office, knowing that I am the rare colleague who does not eat the cake she brings to work. (Avoiding cake between 9:30 A.M. and 6:00 P.M. is one of the few dietary restraints I manage to observe.) In truth, I do not have to eat Melissa's cakes to appreciate the joy they bring to the staff of our program. For a producer, editor, or booker, partaking of a home-baked Melissa Gray cake every week is a palpable bonus of working on the program, a good thing since real bonuses are precious few and far between. Melissa's art school training is also in evidence: her cakes look terrific.

In *All Cakes Considered*, I am delighted to read, at long last, Melissa's long form writing about her baking projects. Like all of her colleagues, I am already familiar with the short form, the Monday morning e-mail message that describes what is freshly baked, edible, and sitting on the producer's desk: "I wanted to make up something slightly different. It's Cinnamon Almond Coffee Cake, using Saigon cinnamon, which is a bit more kicky than regular cinnamon, which is not really regular cinnamon." "ANOTHER version of the lemon-blueberry swirl that I've been working on for two weeks now. Changes this time involve folding meringue into the batter and adding (GASP) a sprinkle of coconut over the blueberry before layering and marbeling. Dig in. And no complaints about the coconut." "Up front is another attempt at that *&^%$# Cinnamon Almond Coffee Cake."

These messages leaven the typical traffic of news reports, press releases, and sightings of earrings left in the fourth-floor ladies room that clog our desktop computers. They remind me that people who work together are a potential community, capable of sharing in some of life's delights without distracting anyone from the tasks of the office. They are, of course, equally capable of being nine-to-five sharp-elbowed, paranoid snipers who steal one another's ideas and office supplies. Of such colleagues I say, "Let them eat cake, baked according to Melissa Gray's impressive and dependable recipes." They will be better human beings.

Robert Siegel
Host, All Things Considered

POSTSCRIPT TO THE FOREWORD: INSKEEP'S REBUTTAL

Robert Siegel is a respected colleague, a perfect dinner companion, a great reporter, and the Walter Cronkite of our time—the man who informs me who's winning on election night. Is that enough flattery for me to get away with calling him a dang fool? How could he not sample the cakes described in this book?

Granted, Robert made a thoughtful decision to refrain. I never think about Melissa's cake. I just eat it. I step into the studio for some interview with the ambassador from Belarus, and when I return to my desk, there is a paper plate with a slice of cake resting on my chair. Is Melissa the source of this cake? I don't ask such questions. I just assume it's another of life's little bounties, which is probably the same thing a mouse thinks in that final half second before sticking its nose in the trap. But the trap hasn't closed yet; and if all this cake means I'll be swimming another few thousand laps in the pool, then I will thank Melissa Gray for making sure I live my life to the fullest. Show this book to a loved one. Maybe you, too, can get frosting on your chair.

Steve Inskeep
Co-Host, Morning Edition

So, you want to bake a cake,

HUH?

AND YOU'VE GOT HUNGRY COLLEAGUES, TOO? TWO BIRDS, ONE STONE. CONGRATULATIONS, YOU'VE BOUGHT THE RIGHT BOOK.

PREPARE TO BECOME VERY POPULAR AT WORK. NOT FOR YOUR BRAINS. NOT FOR YOUR BEAUTY. FOR YOUR BUNDT PANS.

I know this to be true.

Every Monday, I bring in a cake for my colleagues at NPR, a.k.a., National Public Radio. Why Monday? Because no matter how much you love your job, Monday is the day you look forward to the least.

There's something about having cake at work that makes everybody happy, even the dieters who proclaim that you're doing this just to torture them. It's a communal thing and a sensory thing. A behavioral psychologist might say that it's using an object (sweet food) to stimulate pleasure receptors in the brain, thus building a powerful association in the subject's mind between work and pleasure.

I hate being analyzed by the likes of B. F. Skinner, so I'll just go Forrest Gumpian: "Momma says cake brings people together."

And why not have cake on the job? The average American worker spends between eight and ten hours a day with a group of people to whom he or she is unrelated. It's not your family, yet a great bulk of your energy and brainpower goes toward supporting this group. Being at work can either drain you or stimulate you. Though I just dissed B. F. Skinner, I'd rather be stimulated, thank you very much. This is why I work at NPR. Not only is the work rewarding, exciting, and fun, but the people I work with are smart, interesting, comical, and warm. The longer you work there, the more you become family. I'm Southern, so the thing my family does to show their love is fight and eat. Rather than fight, I bring in cake every Monday.

And, because I'm Southern, there's always more to the story. I could have just brought store-bought cakes to the office every week, but where's the fun in that? No, when this baking thing started, I had a need myself. For most

of my adult life, I only had three good cake recipes, which sometimes turned out well. Two were family favorites, the other was a simple apple cake from Paula Deen that a drunken monkey couldn't screw up. When I took those in to work, most nonbakers were impressed, but I knew my baking was nothing compared to what my mother, aunts, great-aunts, and grandmothers could do. Or did.

We're down to just my mom and a few aunts now, and everybody's on a diet, so the desserts at family gatherings aren't as rich and thrilling and sinful as they used to be. No rum cakes. No sour cream pound cakes. Aunt Di's bittersweet-chocolate frosted layer cake is sadly a thing of the past. And (sorry, Momma) Splenda does not taste as sweet as sugar.

My brother, irritated into action, gave me an expensive tube pan for Christmas one year. It's the identical twin of the one he'd bought for himself. I took it as a not-so-subtle hint that the torch was being passed to a new generation. Except in our case, the torch was a cake pan.

He began a pursuit of all things pound cake, adding blueberries to the batter, mixing in flavored yogurt, trying different kinds of nuts. His wife and stepdaughter were impressed. So were his hunting buddies.

I wasn't interested in doing pound cake, though. Instead, my odyssey began with an ambitious recipe: Martha Washington's "Great Cake."

It's a big, egg-filled creation full of seasonal fruits, plus brandy and pecans, topped with a thin, marshmallow-like layer of frosting. Lots of chopping and mixing. I learned all about this gorgeous beast when I visited Mount Vernon during the holidays. In my tiny kitchen, a few miles north of Mrs. Martha's revolutionary one, I turned on the gas, greased that tube pan, and got down to business.

When the cake arrived at *All Things Considered* (*ATC*), there was collective amazement ("For us? Really?") followed by a chorus of "yummy" noises, rising up in full harmony from the cubicles. The cake wasn't bad. But as I tasted it, I suspected that the icing wasn't right. The crumb seemed way too dense and a little dry; what had I done wrong? And I wondered if almonds might have worked better than pecans with the brandy and pears.

AND THEN I HAD A THOUGHT: I CAN DO BETTER.

My next thought, as I looked at my masticating colleagues, their eyes rolling back into their heads in hedonistic pleasure: ***these people will eat anything.***

THUS OFFICIALLY BEGAN THE CAKE PROJECT.

The rules were simple: a different recipe every Monday. No repeats. No box mixes. No canned frosting. No margarine, no low-fat sour cream, no faux sugar. If a cake bombed, I reworked the recipe and did a "re-cake" later in the week. Recipes came from many sources: family, neighbors, the Internet, newspapers, magazines, cookbooks, cable TV's Food Network, and those spiral-bound collections with the sweet titles and quaint graphics that church ladies put out in every small town.

My main goal was to learn by doing, and when I was ready, I'd re-cake Martha Washington like she'd never been re-caked before.

I had intended the Cake Project to last just three months, but I kept collecting new recipes and new pans. It became six months. Then twelve. It's now an *ATC* weekly tradition, to the point that if I'm out, I arrange for one of my co-workers to fill in, which they do gladly. Word has gotten out in the building, and so we're regularly visited by colleagues from other shows and departments. Sometimes I'll get ideas for my next baking project from interviews we do for the show, conversations we have during the week, or just someone's simple pining for a particular flavor. I know who loves really dark chocolate and who can't stand coconut. And when there's a special occasion, I can now whip up an appropriately festive cake.

I love cake. But I can do without it. What I'm hooked on, and what you'll get hooked on, too, is basking in the joy of simply giving people something delicious to look forward to. Plus, your colleagues are your best and most forgiving test kitchen. They don't care how it looks, as long as it's edible.

If you're a novice baker or you need some recipes that are genuine crowd-pleasers, *All Cakes Considered* is for you. Actually, it's for anyone who wants to bake for other people, but can't find the right cookbook. Believe me, I know. When I first started the Cake Project, I found a lot of cookbooks that seemed calculated to make me feel woefully inadequate, that I had somehow failed as a woman because I'd concentrated on a career rather than mastering home economics. But I also found a few gems that really helped me create some incredible cakes, boosted my self-confidence, and fueled my interest until I eventually learned to improvise on my own. That boost is what I hope to give you, because if I can learn to bake, ANYONE can learn to bake. It's NEVER too late to learn.

In that spirit, here's my first bit of advice: please forget that adage "baking is a science." Yes, yes, the ingredients do react to heat, but read "science" and you think Bunsen burners, asbestos gloves, test tubes, and goggles. Consider this: when you think of chemistry, does the category "relaxing hobby" immediately spring to mind? Chemistry for the average Jane or Joe is intimidating. Baking shouldn't be. It's more about using proper techniques and learning how to follow directions and also trusting your own senses.

How to USE THIS BOOK

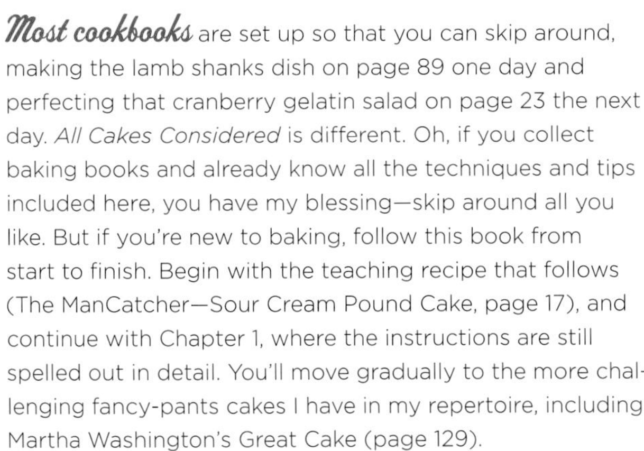

Most cookbooks are set up so that you can skip around, making the lamb shanks dish on page 89 one day and perfecting that cranberry gelatin salad on page 23 the next day. *All Cakes Considered* is different. Oh, if you collect baking books and already know all the techniques and tips included here, you have my blessing—skip around all you like. But if you're new to baking, follow this book from start to finish. Begin with the teaching recipe that follows (The ManCatcher—Sour Cream Pound Cake, page 17), and continue with Chapter 1, where the instructions are still spelled out in detail. You'll move gradually to the more challenging fancy-pants cakes I have in my repertoire, including Martha Washington's Great Cake (page 129).

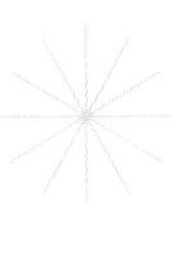

I've set it up this way to help you learn faster than I did when I was skipping around baking books, trying things too advanced for my skill level and getting a wee bit perturbed. See? I'm looking out for ya!

You'll need some EQUIPMENT

We've advanced greatly since the Neanderthals, so you'll need some tools: measuring cups and spoons, a good sturdy hand whisk, plus a stand mixer with beaters and a whisk attachment. I recommend an extra mixing bowl, and smaller, microwave-safe prep bowls. A hand mixer is also a good tool to have. You'll need at least two good rubber spatulas, a 10-inch tube pan, and two 9-inch flat round pans or three 8-inch pans for layer cakes. You'll need some long toothpicks or wooden skewers for testing whether the cake is done, and a good wire rack for cooling. You'll want to buy some baking spray to grease your pans and parchment paper, too: both are gifts of the gods.

We'll dish in detail about ingredients after your first easy adventure in baking. So, thusly armed, away we go, marching on to page 17!

THE MAN CATCHER—
SOUR CREAM POUND CAKE

Your Introduction to Cake Baking

IN THE 1950s, MY GREAT-UNCLE PRESENTED MY GRANDMOTHER WITH A TWELVE-SIDED TUBE PAN. FOR AS LONG AS I CAN REMEMBER, THAT WAS THE SHAPE OF HER SOUR CREAM POUND CAKE. SHE'D BAKE IT LONG ENOUGH TO PRODUCE A MEDIUM-BROWN CRUST. THE INSIDE WAS ALWAYS BRIGHT YELLOW, SPRINGY, AND MOIST.

I call this cake the Man Catcher because, really, no man can resist it. Oh, he might be able to resist YOU, but not this cake: it's really good, but it's no Love Potion No. 9. There are, however, seven secrets to creating the Man Catcher: Measuring, Creaming, Beating, Beating, Beating, Greasing, and No Peeking.

Sounds kind of sexy, I know, but it's still not going to guarantee you a love life. It will, however, provide you with an excellent introduction to cake baking.

YOU'LL NEED

A 10-inch tube pan

- 2 sticks (1 cup) unsalted butter, at room temperature
- 3 cups sugar
- 5 large eggs
- 3 cups all-purpose flour
- ¼ teaspoon baking soda
- ½ teaspoon salt
- 1 cup sour cream
- 1 teaspoon vanilla extract
- 1 teaspoon lemon extract
- 1 teaspoon orange extract

In general, the quality of your cake depends on the quality of your ingredients, your mixing technique, and the right length of time in the oven. So, before we get down to setting the bait to catch our man, let's internalize a couple of rules. The FIRST and most important of all is this:

One

ALWAYS READ YOUR RECIPE BEFORE YOU BEGIN.

Heck, read it BEFORE you go to the grocery store for your ingredients. Why? I'll tell you why: You need to make your list o' things to get, AND you need to go over your list o' what you already got. Inventory yourself: Do you have salted butter or unsalted? You want unsalted. And if you have it, how old is it? Unless it's frozen, it won't last as long in the refrigerator as you might expect. Nor do eggs. And what size eggs are those, anyway? They should be large. Forgot to pick up enough sugar? Don't even think you can substitute confectioners' sugar. And that flour you have smartly stored in the refrigerator? If it's self-rising and you use it for this cake, oh, expect some problems. And speaking of problems, lurking in your pantry is a tin of baking powder from two years ago—roughly the last time you tried making a cake. It's probably deactivated by now. Its only purpose is to lull you into a false sense of security, then crush your cake-baking will. Smell your flavorings: are they still liquid? Anything unpleasant?

Another reason you want to read through your recipes before you begin: you want to understand what techniques you'll be using to make said cake. If there's something you don't know, or aren't clear about, it's time to get online and Google it or, better yet, call a friendly, experienced baker.

HERE ARE THE DIRECTIONS FOR GRANDMA GRAY'S SOUR CREAM POUND CAKE, ALMOST EXACTLY AS SHE SCRAWLED THEM ON AN INDEX CARD, WITH ONLY A FEW CHANGES FOR CLARIFICATION:

Sour Cream Pound Cake

Center rack in oven and preheat to 325 degrees F.
Prepare a pan.
Cream butter and sugar.
Add eggs.
Sift together flour, baking soda, and salt in a separate bowl.
Alternately add flour mixture and sour cream.
Add extracts. Beat until flavorings are incorporated and mixture looks smooth and even.
Pour batter into prepared pan.
Bake 90 minutes.

There's a lot of baking shorthand in this. What does "cream" mean? Do I add the eggs all together? How do I combine the dry ingredients? What's a tube pan? How does it get greased? Is the cake absolutely done at 90 minutes?

So many questions, grasshopper. But Grandma Gray is not alone; many recipes assume you know exactly what they're talking about.

Two

"CENTER RACK IN OVEN AND PREHEAT TO 325 DEGREES F."

That's our SECOND important step to making a cake, after we've read over the recipe.

What does "center rack" mean? Take a look at your tube pan. Look at how tall it is—I'm guessing about 4½ inches. When you put that pan in the oven, you want the body of the cake to be as dead center as possible: the better for even baking. Next, look at your rack in the oven and figure out how low or high it needs to be so that your cake goes where it should—in the center of the oven.

"Preheat" means exactly what you think it means. So does 325 degrees F (Fahrenheit).

Three

"PREPARE A PAN."

This is not about sitting down and having a conversation or exam review with your cake pan; it's about getting your pan all nice and greasy. Wouldn't it be heartbreaking to have used fresh ingredients and a proper mixing technique only to have the Man Catcher refuse to rise to its full glory?

For this cake, I specified a 10-inch, basic tube pan (a tube pan has straight sides, tube in the middle). This recipe also works well in a Bundt pan (a Bundt pan has decorative sides, tube in middle. I'll tell you more about the history of Bundt pans later in the book). If you want to try this cake in a 9-inch square pan or a couple of loaf or layer pans, it will work fine, but you'll need to halve the quantity for each ingredient in the recipe and halve the baking time. But a tube pan is the pan of choice for pound cakes as far as I'm concerned, and every baker needs one.

A pound cake, after all, has a dense batter. Originally they were made with a pound of sugar, a pound of butter, a pound of flour, and a pound of eggs; that's why it's called a pound cake. (What, you thought I wasn't going to explain that to you? Oh, ye of little faith.) Large amounts of dense batter tend to bake better in tube pans, simply because that tunnel in the middle gets the heat into the center, thus avoiding the problem of overbaked on the outside, under-baked on the inside. We don't like gooey when a lot of eggs are involved. That's not just a baking faux pas, it's an icky no-no.

A word about PANS

Not all tube pans are made equally. Some are aluminum, some are coated, some are heavy, some are made of silicone and can be rolled up and stored with little fuss. Others may disagree, but I HATE silicone pans and don't recommend them. I've never had a cake come out of one in the proper shape (it turns out oblong, rather than round) and the silicone pan didn't release the cooled cake without pulling chunks off. So, just say "no" to silicone.

Also, say "no" to el cheapo pans: After ten or twelve cakes, I've found bits of the pan's coating on my cake crumb. Teflon is not an ingredient I want to serve to my co-workers. If you plan to bake more than five times a year, every year, spend the money and invest in at least one good tube pan and one good Bundt pan. Depending on the brand and design, you'll spend between $25 and $50, and it will last you for decades and maybe a lifetime. You want a 10-inch tube pan that holds at least 16 cups of batter. If you go the decorative Bundt pan route, you'll likely end up with a 10-inch that holds only 12 cups of batter. No big whoop: If you end up with excess batter, you can always pour the leftover into a small baking dish and bake up a test cake along with your big cake (a cake just for you! or the mailman). Later, after you've collected a bunch of pans, you may forget how many cups they hold. Again, no big whoop: Just measure out water by the cupful, pouring each into the pan, counting as you go, until the pan is full.

If you're using a traditional tube pan that's flat on the bottom, you can line the bottom with parchment paper. You just put the pan, bottom down, on the paper, trace the outside, then trace that hole on the inside, remove the pan, and cut out the large donut you just made. Place it in the bottom of the pan.

Traditionally, you'd now take the wax paper that was once wrapped around your butter and grease the inside of your pan, including the parchment liner, and then sprinkle flour all over the bottom and sides. But sometimes, tradition needs to go away. Pam makes this great baking spray that includes flour. There's also another brand called Baker's Joy. I love this stuff. I'm tempted to use it as deodorant and hair spray, but it's not really designed for that. Spray your tube pan (or Bundt pan, if you're using that instead), including the center column.

Four

"CREAM BUTTER AND SUGAR."

Creaming is the process of dissolving the sugar into the fat. Your goal is to have a creamy-looking mixture. That's why it's called creaming. D'oh!

Your first impulse might be to unwrap and dump 2 cold, hard sticks of unsalted butter into the mixer, followed by 3 heaping cups of granulated sugar. Your second impulse would be to crank up the mixer and stand back. Your third impulse would be to sing "Babaloo," because that's the weird rhythm you're going to hear as the 2 cold, hard sticks of butter tumble around the mixer on high speed over 3 heaping cups of granulated sugar.

I like Desi Arnaz, but those impulses are all wrong. A full-blown baking NO NO NO. You'll end up with big chunks of sugar-covered butter. It will not be creamed. You will have failed. Resist those impulses (except for singing "Babaloo," I say go for that one) and do this instead (it's a secret most recipes don't spell out for you):

At least 1 hour BEFORE you're ready to begin baking, set out your butter and eggs. You want them at room temperature, because that's going to make creaming sooooo much easier. Ideally, your butter should be soft enough so that you can make an indentation in the stick by pressing on it gently with your finger.

Cut your room-temperature butter into tablespoon-sized pats and put these pats in the mixing bowl. Start your engine and mix for 1 or 2 minutes at medium speed until the butter is smooth and no longer resembles a pile of solid yellow squares.

Next step: you're going to measure out your sugar. Not heapin' helpings, either—you're going to use the *dip, scoop,* and *level* method: Dip your cup into your bag or container, scoop it up, then, holding the cup above said bag or container, run a knife, or your finger, over the top of the cup to *level* it off.

Using this method, measure out 3 cups of sugar and put them aside in a prep bowl. Working from your prep bowl, measure ½ cup of sugar, add it to the butter, and beat for 1 minute on medium speed. Continue adding the sugar this way until all 3 cups are thoroughly creamed (that's 6 half cups and 6 minutes of beating).

Ooooooh, drives you crazy, doesn't it, the time this takes? Remember: the goal here is to dissolve the sugar into the fat. Room temperature and time are your BFFs (that's "best friends forever" for those of you who don't text).

Five

"ADD EGGS."

That means one at a time, mixing to incorporate the egg into the batter before adding the next one. And about those eggs: there will come a time when you've cracked a henhouse full and you've mastered the crack-'em-on-the-side-of-the-mixing-bowl-with-the-mixer-still-running maneuver, but until you've hit that stage of maverick derring-do, STOP the mixer and GENTLY crack open each egg. The LAST thing you want are crunchy bits of shell in your cake, and the second-to-last thing you want to do is waste valuable time and energy fishing out tiny bits of shell from your batter. We all know. We've all done it at least once. It's OK. We've all since promised to do better with our batter.

If you're going crazy just standing there, waiting while you cream each egg with the butter, you have my permission to multitask. This is why I prefer a stand mixer: it frees up my hands for other things. Set a timer for 1 minute after each egg addition and while you're carefully creaming, you can measure out and sift together your dry ingredients.

Six

"SIFT TOGETHER FLOUR, BAKING SODA, AND SALT IN A SEPARATE BOWL."

And about that sifting: Modern flour milling methods give us lump-free, fluffy flour, so traditional sifting (using a nifty hand sifter, THEN measuring out from what you've sifted) is not usually necessary. Life has gotten easier for us in this twenty-first century, hasn't it?

I take a hand whisk and whisk my flour, be it in the container or the bag, as precautionary fluffing: This is because flour settles and sometimes it can get lumpy. Next, I measure the flour into a separate bowl the way I measure sugar: *dip, scoop,* and *level*. I then measure out my other dry ingredients into that bowl and whisk together. No big whoop. And it's fun in a "Look at me! I'm not using a sifter! I'm CHEATING!" kind of way.

Seven

"ALTERNATELY ADD FLOUR MIXTURE AND SOUR CREAM."

You've got about 3 cups of the flour mixture and 1 cup of sour cream to work with, and you want to gradually add these to the creamed mixture, so everything gets nice and evenly mixed together. So . . .

Shift the mixer to the lowest speed. Add about 1 cup of the flour mixture and mix to incorporate. Stop the mixer and scrape down the sides of the mixing bowl with a spatula. Add ½ cup of sour cream. Switch to medium speed and mix until incorporated. Stop the mixer. Repeat, ending with a final addition of about 1 cup of the flour mixture.

Again, you're taking your time with this step because you want nice, even distribution. You're also beating air into that batter, which will ultimately help the cake stand nice and tall.

Eight

"ADD EXTRACTS. BEAT UNTIL FLAVORINGS ARE INCORPORATED AND MIXTURE LOOKS SMOOTH AND EVEN."

In this case the flavorings are vanilla, lemon, and orange extracts. I add one extract, give the mixer a brief spin, then add another, spin, add the last, and give it one last spin. And then I let the mixer run on medium-high speed for another 2 minutes.

That wasn't so bad, now, was it?

Here's another direction you're going to see a lot in baking:

Nine

"POUR BATTER INTO PREPARED PAN."

Start pouring the batter, GO EASY, and then, while tipping your mixing bowl over the cake pan, use your spatula like a border collie and herd the batter that's coating the sides and bottom of the bowl into the main pour stream. Pour the batter against only one side of your pan and let it lava its way to the other side. You don't want any big air pockets getting in there. Air pockets range from pea size to plum size. They can disrupt the baking process and leave craters in your finished cake. (Air bubbles, which help the cake rise, are much smaller—from microscopic to the size of an eraser.)

Do not—DO NOT—fill your tube pan to the rim. NO NO NO NO. Remember, this cake is going to get all patriotic and stand up tall, what with all the air bubbles we've beaten into it during our prolonged mixing process. Fill the pan no higher than 1 ½ inches below the rim. Using your spatula, even out the batter in the pan. If you suspect air pockets, just tap the sides of the pan a couple of times and wait for a belch from the deep.

Ten

"BAKE 90 MINUTES."

(If you make a test cake with leftover batter, it will need to come out of the oven 30 minutes earlier than the big cake. Put the test cake on a lower rack toward the side of the oven. Centering does not apply to test cakes when you're also baking a bigger one.)

Now, "Bake 90 minutes" does not mean "open the door every 15 minutes to make sure the cake hasn't escaped." No. This brings me to another instruction I want you to burn into your cerebral cortex: Do not molest the cake while it's in the oven. Do not open the oven door. Do not even THINK about opening the oven door. Cakes are shy by nature. They get embarrassed very easily and will collapse like fainting Southern belles under your greedy, lusty gaze.

True confession: constantly "checking" the cake was once one of my worst baking habits (in addition to "creaming" entire sticks of cold butter with all the sugar at one time). Every time the oven door opens, it lowers the oven temperature, causes vibrations, and disrupts the rise of the batter. It's a great way to get a heavy, thick, fallen cake and no happy cake dance for you.

If I'm worried about cake batter overflow, I make sure to line the bottom rack of the oven with aluminum foil before the cake pan goes in. Better yet, I don't fill my pans too high. But I do not even consider opening the door unless it's 10 minutes before the timer will go off or I smell smoke. The oven gods have been kind, and I've had few fallen cakes since adopting this habit.

Here's a tip for all you aspiring Martha Stewart perfectionistas: don't stomp around the kitchen while your cake is baking. Proceed with your cleanup placidly and calmly, like you're on Prozac or Valium and everything is fine, fine, fine with the stock market. Make your kitchen a no-fly zone if you have kids, pets, or inquiring partners, too.

Let me tell you a story while you're filling the sink with hot, sudsy water. Papa, my mother's father, LOVED fallen cakes. Some people do. When he was a boy, during the Depression, his job was to keep the kitchen stove going. That meant adding wood every so often. If a cake was baking, he'd DROP the wood into the fire box extra hard and SLAM the door for good measure, hoping the vibrations would result in a fallen cake. And often he was a lucky boy, indeed. Not sure how his momma felt about it.

HOW TO TELL YOUR CAKE IS DONE AND HOW TO GET IT OUT OF THE PAN

Beep! Beep! Beep! Your timer just went off. Get a long toothpick, a thin skewer, or a knife and have it at the ready.

Using oven mitts, pull your oven rack about halfway out of the oven, exposing half of your cake, which, as you recall, is centered on the rack. Poke your toothpick, thin skewer, or thin knife into the middle of the cake ring. If it comes out clean, your cake is done. If not, back in the oven with it for 10 minutes (15 if it comes out gooey), then retest. Continue doing this until your toothpick or knife comes out clean.

Why not pull the whole pan out of the oven rather than pull out the rack? Remember what I said about fallen cakes? Yeah. Exactly. If your cake is not quite done, you're risking a fallen cake by manhandling the pan into much cooler air.

Tip: Here's something experienced home bakers will tell you, but many cookbooks won't: as you bake more, you'll get to know your oven. I bake in a small, apartment-sized gas oven. It's a slow oven. Often, recipes that say "90 minutes" will take me 10 more minutes. If the windows are open in the house and there's a breeze blowing, it will take even longer. It's just the way my oven is, and yes, I dream of replacing it one day. But I've learned how to compensate for its slacker ways. My father-in-law has an electric oven and it's fast. When a recipe says "90 minutes," I visually check the cake at 75 minutes. Fortunately, he has a glass window, so I don't have to open the door and startle the cake. My mother's oven is just right: if a recipe says "90 minutes," usually the cake is ready at 90 minutes. But my point here is this: Get to know whether you have a slow oven, a fast oven, or a just-right oven and take that knowledge into account, Goldilocks, when a recipe tells you "bake 90 minutes."

When the cake tests done, remove it from the oven and let it cool in the pan for 15 to 30 minutes. When the cake has pulled away from the sides of the pan, and the pan is touchable, it's time to remove the cake. Here's how: if your cake is in a straight-sided pan, take a butter knife and gently run it all the way around the inside, loosening up any cake that's stuck.

If it's in a decorative Bundt pan, skip the part with the knife. I hope you did a mighty fine job with the baking spray 2 hours ago.

Getting back to the straight-sided tube pan: If you like the way the top of the cake looks, all brown and dome shaped with little cracks showing a slip of moist yellow crumb (oops, sorry—that's a little cake pornography there), get a sheet of parchment paper to cover the top. Get a plate. Invert a cake rack onto top of pan. Place one hand squarely under the pan and the other hand squarely on top of the inverted rack. In one easy motion, flip the pan so that the rack is now holding the weight of the cake. You may hear a tell tale *thwump* as the cake drops to the rack.

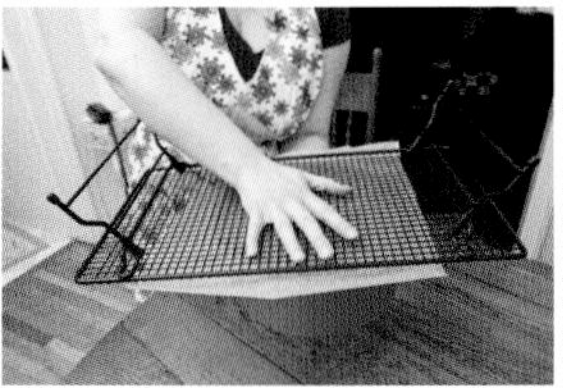

Put the rack on a table or counter and gently lift your cake pan slightly—it may require a very small shake to fully unmold the cake. Peel away the parchment paper. Next, take your plate and place it upside down on your upside-down cake. Again, with one hand squarely on the plate, then the other on the rack, squarely over the cake, flip your cake in one easy motion. Let the cake cool before before covering.

If you're using a Bundt pan, then the top of your cake will actually become the bottom. If it's too dome shaped, you'll want to get a long, serrated knife and level the cake off—this has the added bonus of giving you something to snack on right away. (If you're using a tube pan and you don't like the look of the top of your cake, treat it the same way.) After you've trimmed it to make the top (really, the bottom) flat and even, get your serving plate or cake rack, place it upside down over the top of the Bundt pan, place one hand squarely on the inverted plate, the other under the pan, and flip your handful in one easy motion. Listen for that *thwump* sound. Place the plate on the counter and lift up the cake pan very slightly. In a few seconds, the cake should drop easily onto the cake rack and you can remove the pan. Remember—a small shake if it seems stuck. Cool to room temperature, transfer to a plate if needed, and serve.

WHAT? MORE INFO?

Sour cream pound cake freezes well, but you might want to slice it before freezing—defrosting will take less time that way, plus you can take out only the amount you plan to serve.

VARIATIONS

When this recipe was originally published back in the '60s, it came with several variations, and readers were encouraged to choose their favorite version. You could, for example, use 1 cup of whole milk instead of sour cream. You get a sweeter cake that way, though it's not as moist or tangy.

My whole family has played around with this recipe from time to time. In the "choose your own" spirit, we have the following suggestions, which can be used one at a time, or mixed and matched, depending on what you like:

Blueberries: Add 1 cup of blueberries, but since they break easily, coat them with flour first. My brother puts the flour and blueberries in a zipper-top plastic bag and carefully shakes it, with his pinkies extended. Add the blueberries gently to the finished batter and mix carefully with a spoon or spatula, NOT with the beaters or paddle.

Cherries: Add 1 cup of pitted fresh cherries, coated, like the blueberries, with flour.

Dried cherries or raisins: Add 1 cup of dried cherries or raisins; you don't have to be gentle. You can just run the mixer on its lowest speed for a couple of rotations, until the dried cherries or raisins are mixed in.

Pecans or other nuts: Add 1 cup of chopped pecans using the same method as for dried cherries and raisins.

Flavored yogurt: Ahhhh, the tartness of sour cream, plus an additional flavor from the dairy section. I'd stick with the fruit yogurts, though, because the idea of coffee-flavored yogurt going into this cake makes me gag. My favorite flavor for this cake is cherry vanilla. My brother has tried it with cherry cheesecake–flavored yogurt. He didn't like it, but he's a pound cake fundamentalist. His wife and her fellow teachers liked it well enough to ask for more. Whatever flavor you choose, replace the 1 cup of sour cream with 1 cup of yogurt.

Lemon glaze: Mix 3/4 cup of confectioners' sugar with 1 1/2 tablespoons of milk and 1 teaspoon of lemon extract (or 2—taste it, see how much tartness you want). Beat until smooth and drizzle over the top of the cooled cake.

And you thought you were just learning one cake. Darlin', congrats! You've now got at least seven! Not only have you learned the basics of making a typical cake; once you've taken it to work, you'll become office hero for the day!

True cake LORE

In many traditions, if you find a coin or some other trinket baked into a ring-shaped cake, it's considered good luck. King cakes—those yeasty, cream-cheese-and-praline-filled cakes drizzled with colored sugar that are eaten during Mardi Gras—have a little plastic baby inserted inside. The person who gets the baby has to bring the cake the next year.

Well, my pal Marguerite Nutter, a baking novice, decided to give this sour cream pound cake recipe a whirl for Thanksgiving with her mom, stepfather, and sisters. The cake looked beautiful (she was so proud, she sent me a picture from her cell phone), and she said it tasted great! And there was a surprise in it, too: the silver-foil seal from her brand-new bottle of vanilla extract. When her five-year-old nephew found it, sister Patty said (quick as a flash) "That means you win a prize!" and Marguerite, without missing a beat, handed him a five-dollar bill.

Keep this story in mind if you ever have an alien-object-cooked-in-the-cake mishap.

WHAT'S IN THAT CAKE?

A briefing on ingredients, with tips

SO I TOLD YOU TO FORGET THE ADAGE "BAKING IS A SCIENCE" BECAUSE I DIDN'T WANT YOU TO GET OVERLY ANXIOUS. BEFORE YOU CONTINUE BAKING, THOUGH, I'D LIKE TO BRIEFLY EXPLAIN A FEW THINGS SO THAT YOU UNDERSTAND WHY EVERYONE ALWAYS SAYS "BAKING IS A SCIENCE."

Flour, sugar, fat, and eggs are the basic building blocks of cake. They're most often helped by leavening agents, salt, and flavorings. What begins in your mixer and finishes in your oven is a chemical reaction, albeit a tasty one. Let's get molecular for a moment.

Liquids in your batter, when heated, produce gases with wanderlust: They don't want to stay put in a cake-pan prison—they want to escape into the freedom of the atmosphere. Some gas is already present in your batter before it even hits the oven: Air, which is a mixture of gases (about 78 percent nitrogen and about 21 percent oxygen), is introduced when butter and sugar are creamed and when the other ingredients are mixed in. And carbon dioxide is created when a leavening agent, like baking soda or baking powder, reacts to liquid in the batter. When the batter is heated, the air and CO_2 are trapped by weblike structures formed by proteins in flour and eggs. During their jailbreak attempt, the gases pull those protein structures up with them—that's how a cake rises. Any anomalies in your ingredients, your mixing, or your baking can disrupt that process.

And now for the ingredients. In the baking aisle of your friendly neighborhood grocery store (also home to those damnable cake mixes), there's a variety of different flours, sweeteners, and fats.

FLOUR

Flour is generally made by milling the kernel of soft and hard wheat. There are flours made from rice or soybeans, but they're not ideal for baking cake.

Bread flour is made from hard wheat and is high in protein, about 14 percent. It's used in making cakes that are leavened with yeast, like kugelhopf.

All-purpose flour is a combination of hard and soft wheat, and has a protein content of about 10 percent. It's enriched flour that's usable in all cake recipes, and preferable in cakes with fruits and nuts because it provides a stronger structure than cake flour. You'll notice two types of all-purpose flour: bleached and unbleached. Bleached is made white by the use of chemicals; unbleached flour turns ivory or light maize in color by exposure to oxygen in the air. These flours are interchangeable. All-purpose flour is usually sold in one-, two-, five-, and ten-pound bags.

Self-rising flour is a flour to avoid unless a recipe specifically calls for it. It's enriched bleached soft wheat flour with leavening and salt added, and is great for biscuits and quick breads. Its rising power can weaken within 6 months, though, so it's an ingredient with an expiration date. If a recipe calls for self-rising flour and you don't have it, just add 1 1/2 teaspoons of baking powder and 1/2 teaspoon of salt for every cup of flour and you should be fine.

Cake flour is made from bleached soft wheat and has the lowest amount of protein—about 4 percent. It absorbs less moisture than other flours, and produces a light, delicate crumb. Generally, it's sold in two-pound boxes. Be sure you don't buy self-rising cake flour in its place.

There are also whole wheat or graham flour and stone-ground whole wheat flour, which are made by milling hard wheat from the entire wheat kernel, shell and all. They're very nutritious compared to white flour; they have a higher protein content, anywhere from 12 to 15 percent, and are full of flavor.

If you decide to fiddle around with a recipe to create a "healthier" cake by substituting wheat flour, realize two things: (1) you're going to drastically alter the taste of your recipe, as wheat flours tend to have a nutty flavor; and (2) you're going to have one heavy cake. Don't replace more than half of your white flour with whole wheat, and be choosey about which recipes you want to try this with (spice cakes, for instance, can work, but not delicate party cakes).

Whole wheat flour can go rancid quickly. If you're not using it within a week, store it in the fridge. It will last up to 3 months there and up to 1 year in the freezer. Just make sure you bring it to room temperature before using it.

You can keep white flours at room temperature for as long as 6 months if they're stored in airtight containers. They'll keep at least 6 months in the refrigerator and 2 years in the freezer. Again, make sure you bring them to room temperature before using.

SWEETENERS

Sugar is made from sugarcane or sugar beets. It not only sweetens your cake but also helps keep it moist, brings air into the batter, stabilizes egg whites, and turns your cake crust all pretty and brown. You can also use sugar to finish or decorate your cake. Stored in an airtight container, sugar has a long self life, but you should always check it for lumps or (ewww!) bugs.

Granulated sugar is also known as table sugar, fine sugar, or simply "sugar." This is usually what you buy when you pick up those one-, two-, five-, or ten-pound bags. It is economical and perfectly good for most cake recipes. Note: In this book, when "sugar" appears in the list of ingredients, it means granulated sugar.

Superfine sugar is more finely granulated. It dissolves very easily, which makes it perfect for mixing with egg whites. It's interchangeable with granulated sugar. It's also more expensive and is typically sold in one- or two-pound boxes. To make your own, you can always put your regular granulated sugar in a food processor and pulse for a minute or two if you need smaller granules or just want the joy of using your food processor.

Confectioners' sugar is also known as powdered sugar or 10-X sugar. It is not generally used in standard cake batters as it's fine and soft and does not aerate as well as granulated or superfine. It is, however, perfect for icings and frostings because it dissolves so well.

Sanding sugar and coarse sugar have large granules and are sprinkled over baked goods as decoration. Sanding sugar has larger crystals than coarse sugar (which has larger crystals than granulated sugar). You can get sanding and coarse sugars in different colors, too, if you're into that sort of thing.

Brown sugar is basically granulated white sugar with the molasses added back in. Molasses is a by-product of the refining process. It's what's left over from the boiled juice of the sugarcane or sugar beets after the sugar crystals have been removed. Light brown sugar has less molasses added back than dark brown. Brown sugar is moist and makes slightly heavier, moist cakes, but with a robust flavor. Since brown sugar is so moist, make sure you pack it in the cup when measuring. And you'll want to store brown sugar in an airtight container. I use rubber bands to seal my brown sugar bags, and then seal them in zipper-top bags.

If you open up your brown sugar at a later point and discover a hard brick o' brown sugar, try this: toss in an apple slice and wait 24 hours. OR simply wet a paper towel, wring it out, and wrap it around the brown sugar brick and place in a microwave-safe bowl. Microwave it for about 20 seconds. Crumble the now revived pieces of brown sugar and repeat with any hard brick parts left over.

Other sweeteners include corn syrup, honey, and the above-mentioned molasses. Corn syrup is made from cornstarch, and there are two varieties: light and dark. Dark has a slight flavor, so light is the preferred syrup for most bakers. The taste of honey depends on what flowers the bees pollinated—the most common are clover, orange blossom, and lavender. Honey will keep for years at room temperature, but it often crystallizes. Carefully warming the jar or bottle up in the microwave on low power for 10 seconds at a time, or gradually heating the jar or bottle in a saucepan of water on low heat will return it to a liquid state. Molasses is generally used in gingerbread and sometimes in spice cakes. Most bakers prefer unsulphured molasses, meaning no sulphur has been used in processing it.

FATS

Fats provide moisture and flavor; solid fats help trap air in your cake batter during creaming.

Butter comes from the cow. Margarine does not. It has the same calories as butter, though it may be lower in cholesterol or cholesterol-free. My cholesterol's fine, so I use butter because I prefer the taste and texture. But you can use margarine if you please.

Use unsalted butter for baking—it's sweeter, and it will allow you to control the amount of salt you use in your cake. It's also more expensive, and it goes bad faster. Stored tightly wrapped, it will keep in your refrigerator for 2 weeks, but freeze it and it will be good for up to 8 months.

The main thing to remember when using butter for cakes is this: when creaming is involved, you want it at room temperature. It should be soft enough so that it will hold the indention when you press down on it with your finger. I know I said that in the previous chapter, but I want you to remember it.

Getting butter to room temperature can take anywhere from 30 minutes to a couple of hours, so you're going to be tempted to find a shortcut. Temptation may present itself to you in the form of a microwave. Try warming your butter for 10 seconds on low power, but you'll have to rotate the butter if your microwave doesn't do that for you—you do not want it to melt. If you have a range-top oven, you can start preheating with the wrapped butter on the range top. Again, you need to remember to rotate your butter. Being that vigilant is a pain in the butt, so I always just leave the butter out on the counter and come back an hour later.

Vegetable shortening is made from hydrogenated vegetable oil. Crisco is probably the most recognizable brand. It will last for a year if it's stored tightly wrapped in the refrigerator. I like to use "stick" shortening—the quotation marks are there because it is so soft that calling it a stick is an abuse of the English language. The beauty of "stick" shortening is that measurements are printed out on the foil wrapper. Use the unflavored shortening, not the butter-flavored variety, for the cakes in this book.

Oils are made from vegetables, nuts, seeds, and fruits. For baking, you want to use oil without a strong taste, like safflower or canola. Oils can go rancid, so taste before using. Canola, if stored away from heat and sunlight, can keep for up to a year. The shelf life of safflower, however, is a sad, fleeting thing—safflower can go bad in 3 months.

EGGS

Eggs hold fat and other ingredients together. When egg whites are whipped to firm peaks and added to batter, they act as leavening agents by trapping air. You'll want to use large eggs for the recipes in this book. Check the carton for cracked ones (you don't want those) and when you get home, put the eggs in the coolest part of the refrigerator, and make sure their little pointy heads are facing down. They have a pretty long shelf life this way, about 4 weeks. But if you're suspicious about your eggs' freshness, try this: place an egg in a bowl of water. If it's a floater, get new eggs.

Like butter, eggs should be brought to room temperature before working with them. But they shouldn't sit out longer than 1 hour. As a shortcut, or when an egg meets an unfortunate, messy end and I need a backup extra egg while creaming, I fill a bowl with tepid water and place my egg in there. It takes the chill off and gets the egg to room temperature in a short amount of time—about 10 minutes.

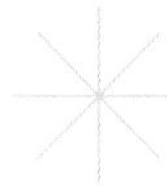

LEAVENINGS

To "leaven" means to add an ingredient that produces gas, which lightens dough or batter. Eggs and butter can act as leavening agents, but there are two others you'll routinely use:

Baking soda is an alkaline powder that works best in combination with acidic ingredients, such as natural cocoa powder, chocolate, molasses, brown sugar, honey, sour cream, yogurt, buttermilk, and citrus juices. It's also very absorbent, which is why people use it in stinky office refrigerators. Store it in a cool, dark pantry and it will generally stay active for about 1 year. If you think yours may be too old, test it by combining 1/2 teaspoon of baking soda with 1/2 teaspoon of vinegar. If you've got bubbles, you're good to go.

Double-acting baking powder may sound like it's the big gun, but it has about a fourth of the power of baking soda. Baking powder contains some baking soda, along with cream of tartar and some cornstarch to absorb moisture. Double-acting baking powder works in two stages: the first occurs when it comes in contact with liquid, and the second happens when it's exposed to heat. It has at least a 6-month shelf life, but may last longer. Think it's too old? Test it this way: add 1 teaspoon of baking powder to 1/2 cup of hot water. Got bubbles? Then you're good to go.

OTHER STUFF

Liquids give those leavening agents a dance partner. Milk is a common addition to recipes (whole milk is preferable but 2 percent is fine). In recipes with chocolate or spices, sometimes coffee or espresso is used. Then again, sometimes all it takes is a cup of boiling water. And although sour cream and yogurt are not liquids, they are moist enough to serve the same purpose.

Cream of tartar is just fun to say. Tartar is a by-product of wine making. It forms on the inside of wine casks during fermentation. It's used in baking to stabilize egg whites and keep sugar from crystallizing while being heated.

Salt provides flavor or enhances it. You can use regular old table salt, or you can use kosher salt.

Vanilla extract is made from vanilla beans, alcohol, and water. It smells great, but tastes bitter, bitter, bitter. It's expensive and there is a synthetic version of it, but I prefer the real stuff. If you're planning to do a lot of baking, buy a big bottle, as you'll use up this flavoring faster than all the rest.

Ground cinnamon, nutmeg, mace, allspice, clove, and ginger are the most commonly used spices in baking. They will keep for as long as 1 year if stored in airtight containers, away from heat and light. Test by smelling and tasting—if they're weak, buy new spices. For details on spices, see page 102.

Chocolate is worth its own book. For baking, you'll use unsweetened cocoa, unsweetened baking chocolate, and bittersweet or semisweet chocolate. And as far as the cocoa goes, there's a potential ingredient trap you should know about: only use Dutch process unsweetened cocoa when a recipe specifically calls for it—otherwise, use regular unsweetened cocoa. The differences between the two are explained on page 75.

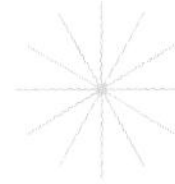

Chapter One

EASY CAKES FOR EARLY ENTHUSIASTS

Brown Sugar Pound Cake HOW COME YA TASTE SO GOOD, NOW?

YOU'LL NEED

A 10-inch tube pan

2 sticks (1 cup) unsalted butter, at room temperature
½ cup shortening
One 16-ounce box brown sugar (light or dark, about 2¼ cups)
½ cup sugar
5 large eggs
3 cups all-purpose flour
½ teaspoon baking powder
1 cup milk
2 tablespoons vanilla extract
1 cup chopped pecans
Cream Cheese Frosting (optional, facing page)

1. Remember our creaming instructions? At least 1 hour BEFORE you're ready to mix, set out your butter and eggs.
2. Position a rack so the cake will sit in the middle of the oven, and preheat the oven to 350 degrees F. Line the bottom of your tube pan with parchment paper and spray the sides and bottom with baking spray. (You can also prepare the pan later, while you're patiently creaming the butter.)
3. Cut up your butter into pats and drop into the bowl of your mixer. Cut your shortening up into 4 parts and add to the bowl.
4. Start your engines and cream the butter and shortening together on medium speed.
5. Combine your sugars together in a separate bowl, then add them, ½ cup at a time, to the creamed mixture, beating 1 to 2 minutes between additions.
6. Add the eggs, one at a time, beating 1 to 2 minutes between additions.

   (See? You learned so well the first time, I don't have to write as much.)
7. While you're creaming or mixing, in your own sweet time, dry whisk your flour and baking powder together in a separate bowl.
8. Once you've added the eggs, slow the mixer down to low speed and add your flour mixture and milk to the batter, alternating between the two. Remember our previous ratio? Add 1 cup of dry ingredients for every ⅓ cup of wet. Beat after each addition. Shift the mixer to medium-high speed and beat for 1 minute more.
9. Slow that mixer slightly and add the vanilla extract. After 1 minute, slow the mixer as low as you can go and add the pecans.
10. Pour the batter into the prepared tube pan and center it in the oven. Bake for 70 minutes or until a toothpick or thin knife inserted in the middle of the cake comes out clean.
11. Cool in the pan for 15 minutes, then remove the cake from the pan using our plate-over-pan method and flip it onto a cake rack (see page 28). Continue cooling the cake.
12. If you like, cover with Cream Cheese Frosting.

Cream Cheese Frosting

I like the Brown Sugar Pound Cake just the way it is, but if you like frosting, or say you bake it a little too long and you know it might be too dry, use this recipe. Just frost the top and let a little drip down the sides. You can get it to drip by just adding extra frosting to the edges and using your spatula to lightly pat down the frosting there.

YOU'LL NEED

1 stick (½ cup) unsalted butter, at room temperature
One 8-ounce package cream cheese, at room temperature
2 teaspoons vanilla extract
One 16-ounce box confectioners' sugar (about 3¾ cups)

1. Using a mixer, cream the butter and cream cheese exactly the way you creamed the butter and shortening for the cake.
2. Add the vanilla extract and beat.
3. Gradually add the confectioners' sugar, the same way you added the regular sugar to the batter, ½ cup at a time. Beat until smooth.
4. Now, if your frosting isn't stiff enough, add a little more confectioners' sugar. If it's too stiff, gradually add a tablespoon of butter or as much as you need to reach the desired consistency. Some people like it stiff, some like it soft. Nobody's right, and it's your cake.

OK, you're learning so well that I'm going to shorthand some of the recipes from here on. Use what you know about creaming, beating, and cooling unless otherwise directed.

A few years ago, when my mom was short on cash but long on time, she jotted down all her favorite recipes on index cards and presented them to me in a photo album for Christmas. It was a very thoughtful gift, especially since she included helpful tips like how to "improvise" brown sugar: you stir 2 tablespoons of dark molasses into 1 cup of white sugar.

This pound cake recipe was in the photo album, and it was among the first cakes I made for *All Things Considered*. It eventually ended up on an index card for Melissa Block, who, despite tremendous self-control, HAD to have a second piece. The office goats will always devour a cake and declare it the "best they've ever had," but if our show's host breaks focus on her work TWICE because of the Monday cake, I know I've got a keeper. And a happy host.

This cake can be sliced thinly, so plan on serving between 16 and 32 people—depending (of course) on how you slice it.

Missy G's Sweet Potato Pound Cake A LESSON IN RE-CAKING

YOU'LL NEED

A shallow baking pan
A potato masher
A 10-inch tube pan

FOR THE CAKE

About 4 medium sweet potatoes
2 sticks (1 cup) unsalted butter
1 cup sugar
1 cup dark brown sugar
4 large eggs
3½ cups all-purpose flour
2 teaspoons baking powder
½ teaspoon baking soda
½ teaspoon ground nutmeg
½ teaspoon ground cinnamon
½ teaspoon salt
½ cup milk
1 teaspoon vanilla extract
1 teaspoon maple flavoring
½ cup peeled and diced Granny Smith apples

FOR THE TOPPING

2 tablespoons cold unsalted butter, cut into pats
2 tablespoons dark brown sugar
¾ cup chopped pecans

CONTINUED —

Re-cake ('rē-kāk) *vb:* to bake a cake a second, third, or fourth time in an attempt to troubleshoot or finesse a flawed or bland recipe.

I hate flawed recipes. I'm in the news business. I embrace clarity. I embrace veracity. I eschew sloppiness. Badly written or incomplete recipes make me nuts. Ingredients cost money. Firing up the oven costs money. Baking and cooking take up precious weekend time. I hate wasting time. I hate wasting ingredients, energy, and money. Ergo, when I find myself struggling with a bad recipe, I get perturbed. Annoyed. A wee bit vexed.

If it's an interesting concept, the recipe, I then launch into *CSI: Kitchen* and try to figure out what makes a good cake go bad.

That's what happened with this sweet potato pound cake recipe. See, my father is the sweet potato king of Gloucester County, Virginia. He is a man obsessed. He has sweet potatoitis, which is incurable. He's been known to plant as many as four 600-foot-long rows of sweet potatoes. Each row has about 200 hills of sweet potatoes. There are about 10 to 20 tubers per hill. Do the math. (Hint: it's a *lot* of sweet potatoes.)

And he's overly generous. I hardly cook, but he usually thrusts two bags of sweet potatoes at me, which I then have to find a place for under the sink, which I soon forget about. And then, when I do remember, half of them have shriveled and sprouted, which just makes me mad because I told him not to give me two bags.

All those Golden Nuggets. All those Beauregards. Gone to spud.

So, I needed baking recipes for sweet potatoes. I have a great sweet potato biscuit recipe. I also have two really good sweet potato soufflé recipes. But I thought, wouldn't it be great to have a sweet potato pound cake recipe?

I found one, and it fell. Three times. Fell despite my attempts to keep it from falling. Three times. I baked it longer, but it was still too moist—it had a steamed pudding texture, rather than a cakeish one. I added ½ cup of flour, but that made it taste more like sweet potato *bread*. And it was bland. To punch it up, I added some flavors from my sweet potato soufflé recipes: I added ½ cup of diced Granny Smith apples, I added ground cinnamon and maple flavoring, and finally, I sprinkled the batter in the pan with a pecan and brown sugar topping. Lord, it was delicious, but the infernal thing fell again.

When in doubt, call Momma. Momma said, "Did the recipe tell you HOW to cook your mashed sweet potatoes?"

"Um, it said 'mashed cooked sweet potatoes,'" I answered.

"I assume you boiled them," she said.

No one knows you like your mother. "I did."

"Don't boil," she instructed. "Bake. Just put them in a shallow pan and bake until they're done. That'll get rid of excess moisture, and it will intensify the flavor. That's what they tell you to do with sweet potato pies. Try it."

Not only was Momma right (Momma's always right), but her tip, plus my previous changes to the recipe, produced one scrumptious cake. The *ATC* staff snarfed the whole thing up, licked the crumbs off their plates, rubbed their bellies, and insisted this was my "best cake ever," "definitely in your top ten of cakes," and they begged, "Can I have the recipe?"

Sure. Here it is. It should serve 20 to 32.

Missy G's **Sweet Potato Pound Cake** — CONTINUED

ABOUT 2 HOURS BEFORE MIXING THE CAKE

1. Preheat the oven to 325 degrees F. Bake your sweet potatoes for at least 45 minutes. Use a knife or a fork to test for doneness—the potato should be very mushy inside its shriveled skin. Remove from oven and cool for 1 hour. Slit each skin lengthwise and remove, leaving the soft, orange center. Mash with a potato masher and measure out 2 cups for this recipe. Cool to room temperature before mixing the cake. If the mashed sweet potatoes are too warm, they will melt the butterfat and the batter won't get as nice and thick as it should.

TO MAKE THE CAKE

2. Position a rack so the cake will sit in the middle of the oven, and preheat the oven to 325 degrees F. Line the bottom of your tube pan with parchment paper, and spray the sides and bottom with baking spray.
3. Cream the butter with a mixer on medium speed.
4. Combine the sugars in a separate bowl. Gradually add to the creamed butter, ¼ cup at a time, beating at medium to high speed after each addition.
5. Add the eggs, one at a time, beating at medium to high speed for 1 minute after adding each one.
6. Reduce the mixer to low speed and add the mashed potatoes, ½ cup at a time.
7. In a separate bowl, dry whisk together the flour, baking powder, baking soda, nutmeg, cinnamon, and salt.
8. In another separate bowl, combine the milk, vanilla, and maple flavoring.

9. With the mixer still on low speed, alternately add the flour mixture and milk mixture, beating after each addition. Start with a third of the flour mixture, beat, then add half of the milk mixture, beat again, and repeat until the last of the flour mixture has been added and beaten in.
10. Turn off the mixer, scrape down the sides of the bowl with a spatula, and then mix the batter on medium to high speed for 2 minutes.
11. Slow the mixer down to the lowest speed and add the apples, mixing until just incorporated.
12. Pour the batter into the prepared cake pan and use the back of a spoon to even out and smooth the batter.

TO MAKE THE TOPPING

13. In a separate bowl (I know—it's like the bowls have Balkanized here), combine the cold butter, brown sugar, and chopped pecans. Mix with a wooden spoon and do not fret because the mixture is crumbly. That's just the way you want it.
14. Sprinkle the topping all over the surface of the batter.

    Bake in the oven for 1 hour and 15 minutes before testing for doneness. Then use a sharp knife to test the cake, and poke it around in a couple of places to determine whether it's finished. This cake can fool ya.
15. Cool in the pan for 20 minutes. Then, using the plate-over-pan method, unmold the cake and flip it onto a cake rack, topping side up (see page 28).

Key Lime Cake

YOU'LL NEED

An 8-inch square or round cake pan, about 2 inches deep (if doubling, two 8-inch cake pans or one 10-inch tube pan)
A grater

FOR THE CAKE

1 stick (½ cup) unsalted butter, at room temperature
1 cup sugar
2 large eggs
1¾ cups all-purpose flour
2 teaspoons baking powder
½ teaspoon salt
⅔ cup heavy whipping cream
1 Key lime

FOR THE GLAZE

½ cup fresh Key lime juice (about 4 limes)
1 cup confectioners' sugar, plus about 1 tablespoon for dusting

TO MAKE THE CAKE

1. Center a rack in the oven and preheat the oven to 350 degrees F. Line the bottom of your pan with parchment paper and spray the sides and bottom with baking spray.
2. Cream the butter with a mixer on medium speed and gradually add the sugar, beating well after each addition.
3. Add the eggs, one at a time, and beat after each addition.
4. In a separate bowl, dry whisk the flour, baking powder, and salt together.
5. Slow down your mixer and add half of the flour mixture to the batter. Beat, then add ⅓ cup of heavy whipping cream. Beat, then add the rest of the flour mixture. Beat, then add the rest of the cream. Beat on medium-high speed for about 2 minutes.
6. Grate the rind of 1 Key lime. Squeeze out about 1 tablespoon of the juice. Add the zest and juice to the batter and beat for 2 minutes.
7. Pour the batter into the prepared pan and bake for 20 minutes.
8. Cover the pan with aluminum foil and bake for another 20 minutes. This prevents the top of the cake from browning and burning.
9. Once the cake is done (you know when—the toothpick, skewer, or thin knife comes out clean when inserted in the middle), cool for 10 minutes in the pan. Remove the cake from the pan using our plate-over-pan method and flip it onto a cake rack (see page 28). Put a plate under the cake rack to catch the drips from the glaze. Take a skewer or a toothpick and poke small holes through the top of the cake.

TO MAKE THE GLAZE

10. You can prepare this while the cake is baking. It doesn't take long at all. Mix the Key lime juice and confectioners' sugar together in a bowl until smooth (I use a hand whisk, but you can do this in the mixer if you so desire).
11. While cake is still warm, spoon the glaze over the cake, allowing time for the cake to soak up the liquid. After you're done, you can reuse the juice pooling under the cake on the plate below the rack to further drench your cake.
12. After the cake has cooled, dust with a little confectioners' sugar and serve.

One of my co-workers, dreaming of getting away to Florida one dreary afternoon, asked if I could bring in a Key lime pie on Monday. "No, I do cake, not pie," I said. "OK, how about Key lime cake, then?" he asked.

Google is a wonderful thing, which is how I found this recipe on www.cooks.com. It's a basic yellow cake. You'll use a toothpick to poke holes through it before drenching with Key lime glaze.

Key lime, named after the Florida Keys, where Ernest Hemingway hung out with his six-toed cats, is also known as Mexican lime, West Indian lime, or bartender's lime. It's smaller, seedier, more acidic, and more aromatic than the more common Persian lime. It also has a thinner rind.

To juice the limes, you can buy a not-so-fancy juicer, but unless you plan to have freshly squeezed OJ or lemonade every couple of days, or you have a cavernous kitchen, you can just as easily juice a lime (or lemon or orange) this way: Cut the lime in half and squeeze each half into a bowl. Then, using the back of a metal spoon, press the inside of the fruit against the rind to extract the remaining juice.

This cake is enough for 8 people when baked in an 8-inch round or square pan. To feed more, use two 8-inch pans or one 10-inch tube pan and double the quantities of the ingredients. If you're using an extra pan, add about 10 minutes to the baking time. For a tube pan, plan on doubling the baking time. And don't forget to write down how long a doubled recipe takes to bake so that you'll know for sure the next time.

Travelin' CAKE

Baking can easily expand your waistline. I burn off my extra calories by taking my cake for a walk before work.

I take the Metro, and it's ten minutes uphill, twenty minutes on the train, and another ten-minute walk through DC's Chinatown before I reach NPR. My cake tags along in a two-part Wilton cake carry; it's made of very sturdy plastic and looks like something out of *The Jetsons*. The plastic cover is molded with a handle on top so it's extra strong. There are three locks that snap the top and bottom of the carry together. I've used my Wilton for years now and NEVER has it come apart in transit. Wilton makes a rectangular one for sheet cakes, too.

Some of my co-workers tell me that their stomachs start growling as soon as they see that cake carry go by, like Pavlov's dogs salivating at the ring of a bell.

I try to keep paper plates and forks stocked at my desk. I also keep a large cake knife at work, too—it's one less thing to carry in.

Once I arrive at *ATC*, I wash my hands, unveil the cake, and cut about 12 slices (about half of a Bundt cake), putting 2 aside for our swing shifters, who don't arrive until hours later. I then send out the Monday cake e-mail. The cake will usually last about 90 minutes, but we like to say "the memory lasts forever." Or at least until the next week.

I was on my way to dinner one Monday night in Chinatown and had my empty cake carry with me. When the hostess at the restaurant saw it, she squealed, "It's YOU!" My dinner companion looked at me and confirmed it was, indeed, me. "No! I see you walking every week with that thing and I always wonder, who gets the cake? And what kind of cake? Misha, look!" She pulled over one of the waitresses, "It's the cake lady!"

There are a lot of characters in Washington's Chinatown. The spinning man, who turns circles in his jogging tights as he moves through the crosswalks; the mumbling Indian menu man, who shoves menus in your face as you wait for the Metro; the Friday afternoon street keyboard man, who plays badly; and now the cake lady. I'm honored.

Procrastinatin' Drunken Monkey Banana Bread

NEW TECHNIQUE ALERT!

PLUMPING DRIED FRUIT WITH RUM

YOU'LL NEED

A 10-inch tube pan
A small saucepan
A kitchen lighter or match

2 cups dried cherries
¾ cup dark rum
2 sticks (1 cup) unsalted butter, at room temperature
1 cup sugar
1 cup light brown sugar
4 large eggs
5 or 6 ripe or very ripe bananas
1¼ cups all-purpose flour
1 cup whole wheat flour
1 teaspoon salt
1 teaspoon baking soda
½ teaspoon vanilla extract
1 cup chopped walnuts

1. Position a rack so the cake will sit in the middle of the oven, and preheat the oven to 350 degrees F. Line the bottom of your tube pan with parchment paper, and spray the sides and bottom with baking spray.
2. In a saucepan on medium-high heat, plump the dried cherries in the rum and flame them.

NEW TECHNIQUE

PLUMPING DRIED FRUIT WITH RUM (IT WORKS WITH BRANDY, TOO!)

Put 2 cups of dried fruit (cherries in this case) in a small saucepan and pour in just enough water to submerge half the fruit, about ¾ cup. Bring to a boil and continue boiling until most of the water has boiled away. Add ¾ cup of rum and leave on the heat for 30 seconds, just enough to warm the rum. Turn off the heat completely. Then, using a kitchen lighter (a lighter with a long nozzle that kind of looks like a gun) or a long match, LIGHT the rum. POOF! You'll have pretty blue flames dancing around the tops of your plumped fruit. Let the flames die (about 2 minutes), then set aside.

3. Cream the butter with a mixer on medium speed. Combine the sugars in a separate bowl and gradually add the sugars, beating well after each addition.
4. Add the eggs, one at a time, beating just enough to incorporate after each addition.
5. In a separate bowl, mash the bananas. Then drain off the slightly thickened water and rum mixture from saucepan into the mashed bananas and stir. Add the bananas to the creamed mixture and beat on medium speed until well blended. FYI: The mixture will not look smooth and creamy. It will look like melted Chunky Monkey ice cream.
6. In still another bowl, dry whisk the flours, salt, and baking soda together. Add to the batter with the mixer on low speed. Add the vanilla extract and mix well on medium speed.

7. Using a spatula or a wooden spoon, stir in plumped cherries and walnuts.
8. Pour batter into the pan and smooth the top with a spatula.
9. Bake for 50 to 60 minutes, or until a toothpick or thin knife inserted in the middle of the cake comes out clean.
10. Cool the cake in the pan for 10 minutes. Remove the cake from the pan using our plate-over-pan method and flip it onto a cake rack (see page 28). Continue cooling the cake on the wire rack.

Ahhhhh, bananas. Remember when they were new? That unblemished, firm yellow skin, pulp perfectly ripe and waiting to be sliced for your morning cereal? Yeah. That was just five days ago, wasn't it? And now you don't want to eat brown bananas, you've really got no time to make banana bread, but times are tight and you don't want to waste them. What's a poor soul to do?

Toss 'em in the freezer. You heard me. Oh, they'll get browner still in there, but the pulp will be perfectly fine. This tip comes from Anita Cater, the wife of *ATC* producer Franklyn Cater. With two kids in their house, I doubt bananas go bad that often, but there must be times when she'd much rather make banana bread *later*. Like next week. Like next week when Franklyn is entertaining the kids while she's cleaning out the freezer. Oh, look! Frozen bananas! Where'd they come from?

Well, freezer surprises happen even when you don't have kids. And when you don't have kids, you can add booze to your banana bread. I learned how to rum-plump dried fruit while producing a figgy-pudding segment for the show with *ATC*'s host Michele Norris and Dorie Greenspan, our favorite baking authority. In addition to making the kitchen smell like flamin' debauchery, rum-plumped cherries really add a kick to banana bread.

To defrost your frozen bananas, simply fill a bowl with warm water and set your chilly bunch in there. Give it about 10 minutes. You'll be able to quickly remove the peel, and though it won't look too pretty, it's far better than watching good bananas turn ugly. This recipe serves 16 to 20, depending on how you slice it.

The Barefoot Contessa's Sour Cream Coffee Cake

CULINARY AND CINEMATIC HISTORY—ALL IN ONE RECIPE!

YOU'LL NEED
A 10-inch tube pan

FOR THE CAKE
1½ sticks (¾ cup) unsalted butter, at room temperature
1½ cups sugar
3 extra-large eggs
1½ teaspoons pure vanilla extract
1¼ cups sour cream
2½ cups cake flour
2 teaspoons baking powder
½ teaspoon baking soda
½ teaspoon salt

FOR THE STREUSEL
¼ cup light brown sugar
½ cup all-purpose flour
1½ teaspoons ground cinnamon
¼ teaspoon salt
3 tablespoons cold unsalted butter, cut into pieces
¾ cup chopped walnuts (optional)

FOR THE GLAZE
½ cup confectioners' sugar
2 tablespoons real maple syrup

1. Preheat the oven to 325 degrees F. Grease and flour a 10-inch tube pan.
2. Cream the butter and sugar in the bowl of an electric mixer with the paddle attachment for 4 to 5 minutes, until light.
3. Add the eggs one at a time, then add the vanilla and sour cream.
4. In a separate bowl, sift together the flour, baking powder, baking soda, and salt. With the mixer on low, add the flour mixture to the batter until just combined. Finish stirring with a spatula to be sure the batter is completely mixed.

Melissa's Note: Don't worry about sifting—dry whisking will work fine.

5. For the streusel, place the brown sugar, flour, cinnamon, salt, and butter in a bowl and pinch together with your fingers until it forms crumbs. Mix in the walnuts, if desired.

Melissa's Note: You can also use a wooden spoon if you don't want to use your fingers.

6. Spoon half the batter into the pan and spread it out with a knife. Sprinkle with ¾ cup streusel. Spoon the rest of the batter in the pan, spread it out, and scatter the remaining streusel on top. Bake for 50 to 60 minutes, until a cake tester comes out clean.

7. Let cool on a wire rack for at least 30 minutes. Carefully transfer the cake, streusel side up, to a serving plate.
8. For the glaze, whisk the confectioners' sugar and maple syrup together, adding a few drops of water if necessary, to make the glaze runny. Drizzle as much as you like over the cake with a fork or spoon.

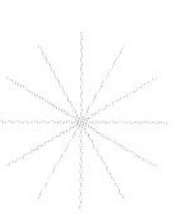

Coffee cakes are different from dessert cakes. They are often stratified by a layer of streusel running through the middle and another one covering the top. I've noticed they are generally less sweet than regular dessert cakes, too, and that makes them good companions to coffee or tea.

Streusel is a German word that means "something scattered or sprinkled"; it refers to a crumb topping made of butter, flour, and sugar, sometimes combined with spices and chopped nuts. You've already made one (the topping for the sweet potato pound cake), so don't panic.

Elizabeth Tannen, a former colleague at *ATC*, spent the bulk of her day at the office negotiating interviews with senators, congresspeople, generals, cabinet secretaries, and the like. She is very persistent, and she lobbied hard for this cake. I'm glad she did. This recipe is considered by many to be one of the best sour cream coffee cake recipes ever. It's by Ina Garten, a former White House staffer who's also known as "the Barefoot Contessa," which is the name of the specialty food store in the Hamptons she bought back in the late '70s, when life in Washington got too dull (it was, after all, the Carter administration and we were living in a fit of malaise). Her first cookbook and her cooking show on the Food Network have the same name, which was itself inspired by the 1954 movie *The Barefoot Contessa*, starring Humphrey Bogart and Ava Gardner.

Gardner (not Garten—it's easy to get them confused) plays a fictional Spanish sex symbol, who marries the love of her life but remains childless because he's got an old war wound. Gardner (again, not Garten; let's not start rumors here) takes a lover and becomes pregnant. But, tragically, her husband kills her and the father of her unborn child.

Hmmm. I think I like this sour cream coffee cake much, much better than the movie.

Many thanks to Ina Garten, who has allowed me to reprint her recipe, originally published in *Barefoot Contessa Parties!*, with my notes. This is a good opportunity for you to read someone else's recipe style while applying what you've learned so far.

This cake serves between 16 and 20 people.

Argroves Manor Coffee Cake

YOU'LL NEED

A saucepan
A 10-inch tube pan

FOR THE STEWED FRUIT

3/4 cup sugar
1/2 cup water
1/2 cup blueberries
1 large apple (Granny Smith if you like bitter, Gala if you like sweet, but NOT Red Delicious!) cored, peeled, and chopped

FOR THE STREUSEL

1/2 cup all-purpose flour
1 1/2 teaspoons ground cinnamon
1/4 teaspoon salt
3 tablespoons cold unsalted butter, cut into pats
3/4 cup light brown sugar
3/4 cup chopped walnuts

FOR THE CAKE

2 sticks (1 cup) unsalted butter
2 cups sugar
2 large eggs
2 cups all-purpose flour
1 teaspoon baking powder
1/4 teaspoon salt
1 cup vanilla yogurt

CONTINUED —

From: Quinn O'Toole
Sent: August 24, 2007
To: Melissa Gray
Subject: Cake!
oh - my - god. I love you from afar.

This cake was the result of a lot of re-caking and a near disaster. I settled on the final version while I was home on leave, recovering from surgery. I sent it in to work and was besieged by a flurry of satiated e-mails later that afternoon.

I'm told it caused a "collective cake-gasm." I would have liked to have seen that.

Here's how I came up with this recipe: One New Year's, at my father-in-law, Bo Argroves's, house in Greenville, Georgia, I was working on a coffee cake, using my *Southern Living* cookbook and the ingredients at hand. There was no sour cream or vanilla extract in the house. But Mr. Argroves's refrigerator was stocked with vanilla yogurt, because that's usually what I have for breakfast. I used that instead. The cake turned out so well, I couldn't wait to try it out on the *ATC* staff when I got back home.

The second time I made it, I got all fancy and added pecans and a little extra yogurt, then baked the cake in a sunflower-shaped cake pan. I was in a rush to get to work, so I didn't test the cake when I pulled it out of the oven, just took a look at the dark brown crust and thought, "That looks done." I showered while it cooled, but later, when I went to unmold it, part of the cake stayed behind in the pan.

Disgusted, I headed for the trash can, but that voice in my head piped up, "Pecans are expensive!" Thrift got the better of vanity, so I wrapped up this embarrassment and into work it went.

And the crowd went wild. They could not believe I was going to throw this cake away. They especially loved the moistness and the nuts.

In the final version, I cut back the yogurt to 1 cup, swapped the pecans for the Barefoot Contessa's streusel (see page 54), and added stewed blueberries and apple to the inside of the cake. I've also moved the cake into a tube pan so it bakes all the way through.

Because yogurt is acidic and there's no additional baking soda in the recipe to neutralize it (remember—there is a little baking soda in baking powder), the cake won't rise high. Instead, it's going to be stocky, but nimble (heavy, but not dense) and rather moist, just a house down from gooey. This recipe saves you from the drudgery of careful beating—you just want to beat your batter enough to thoroughly mix the ingredients, with no worries about getting air into it since it won't rise much anyway. It's a delicious cake, but it's *insanely* delicious when served warm, as you can figure out from Quinn's e-mail.

This cake is best served in thick slices, so plan on at least 16 to 20 cake-gasms.

Argroves Manor **Coffee Cake** — CONTINUED

TO MAKE THE STEWED FRUIT

1. We start with the stewed fruit, which will be ready by the time you're done with the batter and the streusel, in about 20 minutes. Put the sugar and water in saucepan on medium heat. Stir until sugar is submerged, then add the blueberries and apple. Cook for 5 minutes, and reduce the heat to simmer.
2. Continue cooking, keeping a constant eye on the mixture to make sure it doesn't burn, and stirring every 2 to 3 minutes. You want the blueberries to break down in the liquid and the apple to become tender. Once the mixture has become thick, like syrup, turn off the heat and set aside.

TO MAKE THE STREUSEL

3. Dry whisk the flour, cinnamon, and salt together in a bowl. Add the cold butter and brown sugar. Using your fingers or a wooden spoon, combine the ingredients. Knead and crumble until the mixture has an uneven, oatmeal-like texture. Add the walnuts. Make sure the mixture is moist throughout, but crumbly. Set aside.

TO MAKE THE CAKE

4. Position a rack so the cake will sit in the middle of the oven, and preheat the oven to 350 degrees F. Line the bottom of your tube pan with parchment paper, and spray the sides and bottom with baking spray.
5. Cream butter with a mixer on medium speed and gradually add the sugar, beating well after each addition. Add the eggs, one at a time, and beat well after each addition.
6. In a separate bowl, dry whisk the flour, baking powder, and salt together.
7. With the mixer on low speed, add 1 cup of the dry ingredients, followed by 1/2 cup of the flour mixture, beat, then add 1/2 cup of the yogurt and beat again. Repeat once more, beating after each addition. Then beat for 2 more minutes.

TO FINISH THE CAKE

8. Pour half the batter into the prepared tube pan. Using a spatula, spread out the batter evenly. Using a wooden spoon, spoon out the stewed blueberries and apple syrup. Then scatter about three-quarters of your streusel on top. Pour the remaining batter into the pan and smooth it out with a spatula.

9. Move the spatula through the batter in 4 or 5 spots, angling it down, then bringing it up. This will spread the blueberry and apple syrup through to the bottom of the coffee cake.

10. Sprinkle the remaining streusel on top of the batter. Bake for 1 hour and 15 minutes or until a toothpick or thin knife inserted in the middle comes out clean.

11. Cool the cake in the pan for 15 minutes. You'll notice the cake will start falling in. That's OK; that's what it does. Unmold the cake using our plate-over-pan method and flip it onto a serving plate (see page 28). Be careful, as the streusel topping can become loose and go all over creation.

12. Cut thick slices and serve warm.

Miss Saigon Cinnamon Almond Coffee Cake

YOU'LL NEED

An 8-inch square baking pan

FOR THE STREUSEL

2 tablespoons unsalted butter
½ cup dark brown sugar
2 teaspoons Saigon cinnamon
1 cup sliced almonds
2 tablespoons all-purpose flour

FOR THE CAKE

¼ cup shortening
1 cup sugar
2 large eggs
1½ cups all-purpose flour
4 teaspoons baking powder
½ cup vanilla yogurt
1 teaspoon almond extract

TO MAKE THE STREUSEL

1. In a microwavable dish, melt the butter on high power, about 1 minute. Set aside.
2. In a separate bowl, combine the brown sugar, cinnamon, almonds, and flour. Add the melted butter and stir.

TO MAKE THE CAKE

3. Position a rack so the cake will sit in the middle of the oven and preheat the oven to 350 degrees F. When preparing the pan, skip the parchment paper for this one—you may want to serve the cake out of the pan. Do spray the sides and bottom with baking spray.
4. Cream the shortening with a mixer on medium speed and gradually add the sugar, beating well after each addition.
5. Add the eggs, one at a time, beating well after each addition.
6. In a separate bowl, dry whisk the flour and baking powder together.
7. Add a third of the flour mixture to the creamed mixture, beat, then add ¼ cup of the yogurt and beat again. Repeat once more, add the remaining flour mixture, and beat again.
8. Add the almond extract and beat well.

TO FINISH THE CAKE

9. Using your spatula, guide about half of your batter into the prepared pan and smooth it out. Sprinkle a third of your streusel over the batter. Layer the rest of your batter over the streusel and smooth again. Sprinkle the remaining streusel over the batter.
10. Bake for 40 minutes, or until a toothpick or thin knife inserted in the middle of the cake comes out clean. Cool the cake in the pan and serve it straight out of the pan. OR cool the cake in the pan for 10 minutes, then carefully unmold onto a serving plate (see page 28). Remember to cover the top with parchment paper before flipping it over—you don't want the streusel going all over your nice, clean kitchen floors or your nice, clean tootsies.

If you were one of those kids who couldn't wait to chaw on a hot fireball candy, then this coffee cake is for you. It will work fine with regular cinnamon (which isn't true cinnamon; see page 103 for details) but if you do like I do and use Saigon cinnamon, you'll get just a hint of those fireballs that hurt so good.

Saigon cinnamon is the spice used to heat up many a Vietnamese dish. You can find it in any well-stocked grocery store. McCormick, the spice company, sells a potent bottle of it for a little more than what you'd normally pay for regular cinnamon. It's in their Gourmet Collection line.

Now, you may be tempted to turn up the heat on this coffee cake by adding MORE than the recommended 2 teaspoons to the streusel, but my co-worker Graham Smith says simply, "Don't." Graham thinks the ratio of Saigon cinnamon to other key ingredients is just right: too much cinnamon would overpower the yogurty tang of the cake and the smooth almond taste of the streusel. Why would I listen to Graham (other than the fact that I'm paid to listen to Graham, a senior producer, two pay grades up from me)? He's a talented cook and a good baker in his own right. While some of us dash out for salads or burritos at noon, Graham has the most exquisite bag lunches: I've seen him blissfully gnawing on a succulent-looking leg of lamb at his desk more than once. One day, he's going to write *All Lunches Considered*.

This cake serves between 8 and 16.

Dorie Greenspan's Swedish Visiting Cake

NEW TECHNIQUE ALERT!

TOASTING NUTS AND FOLDING

YOU'LL NEED

A round 8- or 9-inch cake pan
A small, shallow baking pan or a pie pan
A cookie sheet

½ cup sliced almonds
1 stick (½ cup) unsalted butter
1 cup sugar, plus 1 teaspoon for sprinkling
Grated zest of 1 lemon (see Tip)
2 large eggs
¼ teaspoon salt
1 teaspoon vanilla extract
½ teaspoon almond extract
1 cup all-purpose flour

Tip: The zest is the sweet outer rind of the lemon—the yellow part, not the white pith. You can also buy dried grated lemon peel in the spice section of some markets, along with dried orange peel. Consider stocking them in your spice collection.

1. Position a rack in the center of the oven and preheat the oven to 350 degrees F. Spray the sides and bottom of the pan with baking spray.
2. Toast the nuts.

NEW TECHNIQUE

TOASTING NUTS

Spread out the nuts, in this case ½ cup of almonds, in a baking pan or pie pan. Put in the oven, preheated to 350 degrees F, for 3 minutes. Using an oven mitt, shake the pan like you would a popcorn bag, and return to the oven for about 3 more minutes. Be very careful not to let them burn!

3. Melt the butter on the stove top or in the microwave on high power and set aside to cool.
4. In a large mixing bowl, combine the cup of sugar and the lemon zest. Blend them, using your fingers (Dorie really likes working with her fingers) or a wooden spoon, until the sugar is moist and smells lemony.
5. Add the eggs, one at a time, whisking after each addition.
6. Whisk in the salt and extracts.
7. Using a rubber spatula, stir in the flour.
8. Fold in the melted butter.

NEW TECHNIQUE

FOLDING

Folding is fun, once you learn how to do it properly. This is not stirring, NO NO NO. You'll need to master this for future recipes, using melted butter or egg whites. I learned how to do this from reading Carole Walter's book *Great Cakes*.

Why fold? When you're combining two things that have different densities (creamed batter and egg whites, for instance), folding ensures that you're blending them together without deflating the egg whites.

Huh, what?

Just like beating your batter, whisking your egg whites introduces air into your recipe. When folding, we're trying to combine the heavier batter with the lighter egg whites and avoid losing that air. Folding is also handy when you want to avoid overmixing: you may want to use it when adding chocolate, nuts, dried fruit, or in this case, melted butter to the aerated batter.

Here's how Carole Walter teaches you to fold: Start with a small amount of what you're adding to the batter, say 1/4 or 1/3 a cup. Then hold a rubber spatula with the curved edge away from you and cut down through the center of the batter. Move the spatula toward you under the batter, running it along the bottom of the bowl, then up the side of the bowl until the spatula is out of the batter.

CONTINUED –

I'd been working at *ATC* for about a year when Dorie Greenspan's book *Baking: From My Home to Yours* showed up in my mailbox; it was sent by a publicist hoping for an interview on the show. Our host Michele Norris had a copy, too, and after I did a pre-interview with Dorie via cell phone, we booked her to talk about holiday baking.

And we fell in love with her. Dorie is adorable: a baking pixie, who's full of great ideas, sage advice, and endless patience. After that one interview, Michele invited her back as a semiregular guest. Together, we and our listeners have learned to bake rugelach, a variation of Katharine Hepburn's brownies, and figgy pudding.

Dorie's books are just as fun and reassuring as she is. It was the first time since I'd started the Cake Project that I'd come across an author who I felt was holding my hand, not talking down to me. I've baked about two-thirds of the recipes in *Baking*, and all of them have been excellent.

This is one of my favorites. Along with my grandmother's sour cream pound cake (page 17), this Swedish visiting cake has become a "satisfies everyone" standby. In fact, it tastes like a Nordic relative of the sour cream pound cake, but it's more almondy than tangy. And it's quick and easy: you don't even need to plug in the mixer.

As Dorie explains, the story behind it is that you could start making the cake when you saw guests coming up the road and it would be ready by the time they settled down for coffee. "They must have long roads in Sweden!" she laughs.

The only thing I tinkered with in this recipe was the almonds: I double the quantity and toast them. I love toasted almonds and figured it was a great opportunity for you to learn a new skill. A warning here: If you're feeding more than 8 people at the office, double the recipe, use 2 round cake pans, and add about 10 more minutes of baking time. I made the mistake of doing a single cake and was faced with a legion of sad, puppy-eyed beggars reduced to scrounging cake crumbs, tearing at their eyes, rending their shirts, and asking, "Why? WHY didn't you bake TWO?!?" So dramatic, I thought the world was ending. This is one problem you run into, doing office cakes—your colleagues' disappointment is proportional to their gratitude.

Dorie Greenspan's **Swedish Visiting Cake** — CONTINUED

Flip the spatula back into its starting position: center of the bowl, curved edge away. With your other hand, rotate the bowl, yes, the bowl, slowly, as you continue to repeat the folding motion with the spatula. Run the spatula around the sides of the bowl every so often.

After one or two full rotations, add the rest of the melted butter, the egg whites, or whatever you're folding in, and repeat. It may take several more full rotations before the folding is done. You'll know, because the batter will be evenly mixed and your arm will be very tired.

9. Pour the batter into the pan and smooth the top with the spatula.
10. Scatter the toasted almonds over the batter and sprinkle with the remaining teaspoon of sugar.
11. Center the cake pan on the oven rack and bake for 25 to 30 minutes, or until golden brown and a toothpick or thin knife inserted in the middle of the cake comes out clean.
12. Cool the cake in the pan for 5 minutes, then run a knife around the inside of the pan to loosen the cake. You can serve it in the warm pan, or unmold (see page 28) and serve on a plate.

Dorie Greenspan's Rum-Drenched Vanilla Cakes

YOU'LL NEED

Two 8 ½-inch loaf pans
A cookie sheet
A sturdy hand whisk
A basting brush (It's like a paint brush, but for cooking.)

FOR THE CAKE

1 stick plus 7 tablespoons (15 tablespoons) unsalted butter
2⅔ cups all-purpose flour
2½ teaspoons baking powder
Pinch of salt
2⅓ cups sugar
6 large eggs
1½ tablespoons vanilla extract
⅔ cup heavy whipping cream
2½ tablespoons dark rum

FOR THE SYRUP

⅓ cup water
¼ cup sugar
¼ cup dark rum

TO MAKE THE CAKE

1. Center a rack and preheat the oven to 350 degrees F. Line the bottom of your pans with parchment paper, and spray the sides and bottoms with baking spray.
2. Melt your butter, either on the stove top or in the microwave on high power. Set aside and let it cool. In the meantime, take out your eggs and bring them to room temperature (about 30 minutes).
3. In a separate bowl, dry whisk the flour, baking powder, and salt together. Set aside.
4. In a large bowl, measure out the sugar and then add the eggs, one at a time, whisking after each addition until thoroughly blended with the sugar.
5. Whisk in the vanilla extract, then the cream, then the rum.

CONTINUED —

This rum-soaked vanilla cake is kind of like pound cake with a "yo-ho-ho" and an "arrrrrrrrgh, Matey." Christopher Turpin, *All Things Considered*'s executive producer, almost fell out of his chair when he tasted his first slice, exclaiming, "OH MY GOD! IT'S RUM! Wow!" I opted not to give Steve Inskeep a slice that day, because he was still on the air with *Morning Edition*. Hey, friends don't let friends eat rum-soaked cake while hosting a national radio show.

Dorie's original recipe called for rubbing the pulp of a pair of moist, pliable vanilla beans into the sugar. That might be a little much since you're just starting out here, so I've just substituted vanilla extract. But I do use high quality dark rum, just as she instructs. This is another recipe for which you don't need to plug in your mixer.

Make the syrup as soon as you get the cakes into the oven—that way the syrup will be cool when you're ready to use it. This recipe calls for loaf pans. Depending on how you slice it, you can get between 10 and 14 servings off a loaf. With 2 pans, that means 20 to 28 servings (nice that I did the math for you, isn't it?).

Dorie Greenspan's Rum-Drenched Vanilla Cakes – CONTINUED

6. Using a rubber spatula, gently add a third of the flour mixture, stirring until just blended before adding the next third. Repeat until all of the flour mixture has been blended in. The batter should be smooth and thick.
7. Fold in half of the melted butter. When incorporated, fold in the rest.
8. Pour the batter into the prepared pans and smooth the tops with the spatula.
9. Place the pans on a cookie or baking sheet and bake. After 30 minutes, check the cakes for color. If they are browning too quickly, take a sheet of aluminum foil and lightly cover them.
10. Bake for an additional 25 or 30 minutes, until a toothpick or thin knife inserted in the center of each cake comes out clean.

TO MAKE THE SYRUP

11. You start by making what's called a simple syrup: Stir the water and sugar together in a medium saucepan over medium heat. After the sugar dissolves, bring the mixture to a medium boil. (Medium, because a full boil will burn the sugar and you do not want that, believe you me). Remove the pan from the heat and stir in the rum. Pour the syrup into a heat-proof bowl to cool.

TO FINISH THE CAKE

12. When the cakes are done, cool for 5 minutes in the pans before unmolding them and transferring them to cake racks. (Remember our technique from the first recipe on page 28? Well, you'll want to flip the loaf pans like you would the tube pan, so the cakes end up with their browned tops facing up, unless you're using decorative molds.)
13. Place the cake racks over a baking sheet lined with parchment or wax paper to catch the drips. Using a thin knife, a long toothpick, or a cake tester (a thin wire you can buy in a specialty cooking store), poke holes through the cake.
14. Slowly brush the cakes with syrup, allowing time for the cakes to absorb the syrup. Leave the cakes on the racks to cool to room temperature before serving.

Of Office Cake and OFFICE CAKE EATERS

You'll notice after you've made several office cakes that your co-workers have definite likes and dislikes. Because of this, I try to keep everybody happy by varying the type of cake I make from week to week. At NPR, here's the breakdown of tastes around the office:

The People's Pound Cake Coalition

This is a conservative group for which there is no other type of cake. They like it moist. They like it heavy. They like its thin, sweet, chewy crust. Try to talk to them about the glories of another type of cake, and they'll pretend they didn't hear you, that a fire truck just passed by, or that you spoke in Urdu (I think one person on staff actually speaks Urdu).

The Chocolate Cake Caucus

Dedicated hedonists and out-of-control addicts, they don't care if it's pudding, pound, or layer, so long as it is *chocolate*. There's no need for interoffice e-mail or a call over the P.A., these people communicate and orchestrate their movements like army ants. They will appear suddenly in one long, continuous line, and they will ravish said cake. There will be nothing left. No crumbs. No icing. One time, even the plate went missing (it's true—I found it in the second-floor pantry the next day, and I swear, it had been LICKED clean). Now, surely you jest, Melissa. Um . . . no, it's been my experience that a chocolate cake at the office will be whittled down to the last quarter slice in less than 30 minutes. Science reporter Joanne Silberner has a lot to do with this. If the CCC ever marches down the block to Capitol Hill in an attempt to overthrow the federal government, arrest her.

The Spice-and-Vice Alliance

Lovers of fruits and nuts join forces with those who relish spice and liquor in their cakes. This is a live-and-let-live kind of group. While they don't share the narrow tastes of the PPCC or the all-consuming drive of the CCC, they do believe in the freedom to hold such narrow views of cake, so long as it doesn't interfere at any time with having apples, walnuts, ginger, or rum in their batter. While membership in the CCC tends to be mostly female, I've noticed that the S & VA members tend to be mostly male.

Now, there are smaller factions of cake eaters, but they're either one-man islands (with mantras such as "I eat NO CAKE BUT ALMOND CAKE!" "COCONUT OR COCO-NOT!" and "IF IT'S NOT GOT SOUR CREAM, IT'S BLOODY WELL NOT FOR ME!"), or they're so congenial that they fall into a broader convention: the big tent o' cake eaters.

These folks just love having cake, any cake, and rather than fight over the flavor (which may result in cessation of all office cake), they just want all of us to get along.

Now, you might think that I'd fall into the big tent o' cake category, given that I'm writing this book and all, but you'd be wrong. While I do generally like all cake (except that spawn of the devil, carrot cake, a recipe that will *not* appear in this book), I'm an unapologetic member of the Spice-and-Vice Alliance.

In fact, if I had a party handle, it would be Ginger. Not because I have red hair, not because I wish I was Spice Girl Geri Halliwell, nor because I wish I were as smart as Ginger Ogren (Gloucester High School, class of 1987). No, it's because my default cake, the thing I'll whip up on a whim, is gingerbread. And that's why there are two recipes for it in this chapter.

Gingerbread, GLORIOUS GINGERBREAD

Gingerbread is easy, and perfect for those midweek office lulls. When the weather's rainy or cold and I think we need a pickup, I'll get up a half hour early and mix up a batch. By the time I've read the newspaper and had breakfast, it's ready to come out of the oven and cool. And by the time I'm out of the shower, it's ready to wrap up and carry in.

Ginger is used in most every cuisine in the world, though gingerbread is primarily a medieval European creation. According to one Web site I visited, the United States has a greater variety of gingerbread recipes than any other country. (I am skeptical of some of the things I read on the Internet: Just how did they determine this? Do the good folks at Pew Research cold-call residents in Sri Lanka, Lithuania, and Peru? 'Cause if Pew president and pollster Andy Kohut wasn't behind it, I may choose not to believe it.)

Now, the use of ginger for flavoring food and for medicinal purposes goes way back to ancient China. And, ginger's not a root, it's a rhizome—a "somewhat elongated, usually horizontal subterranean plant stem that is often thickened by deposits of reserve food material, produces shoots above and roots below, and is distinguished from a true root in possessing buds, nodes, and usually scalelike leaves," according to the Merriam-Webster's dictionary holding up my computer monitor. Bleeding heart plants are rhizomes. But bleeding heart bread doesn't sound too great now does it, smarty-pants?

Ginger's good for what ails ya, if what ails ya is nausea. When I have the flu, I crave ginger ale with crushed ice because that's what Momma used to give me back when I was a wee gal, along with sympathy, chicken noodle soup, and saltines. Western women don't usually eat ginger to counteract morning sickness, but Chinese women traditionally do.

There are some people who are allergic to ginger. They don't break out, they break wind. Or they burp. So if you're one of them, think twice and plan accordingly before trying out these recipes.

Gingerbread

YOU'LL NEED

An 8-inch square or 9-inch round pan

½ cup shortening
½ cup sugar
1 large egg
½ cup molasses (I use dark, or "robust")
1½ cups all-purpose flour
¾ teaspoon salt
¾ teaspoon baking soda
½ teaspoon ground ginger
½ teaspoon ground cinnamon
½ cup boiling water (see Tip)

Tip: OK, you should be able to figure this out, but some rookies don't: You boil MORE than ½ cup of water. When the water reaches the boiling stage, THEN you measure it out.

1. Center a rack and preheat the oven to 350 degrees F. Spray the sides and bottom of the pan with baking spray.
2. Cream the shortening on medium speed and add the sugar gradually, beating thoroughly after each addition.
3. Add the egg and beat until incorporated. Add the molasses and beat until incorporated.
4. In a separate bowl, dry whisk the flour, salt, baking soda, ginger, and cinnamon together.
5. Add half of the flour mixture to the creamed mixture, beat at medium speed until blended, and then add the boiling water. Beat again, then add the remaining flour mixture and beat until smooth.
6. Pour the batter into the prepared pan and bake for 35 to 40 minutes, or until a toothpick or thin knife inserted in the middle of the cake comes out clean.
7. Cool the cake in the pan for 10 minutes. Remove the cake from the pan using our plate-over-pan method and flip it onto a cake rack (see page 28). Continue cooling the cake.
8. Serve and make 8 to 10 of your friends very friendly indeed, or curl up in your La-Z-Boy and eat alone with your cat.

This comes from my well-worn 1971 edition of *Better Homes and Gardens New Cook Book*. Momma picked up a copy of it at a yard sale when she was collecting things for my first apartment. It is a hoot from the very beginning: "Dear Homemaker: From cover to cover, this *Better Homes and Gardens New Cook Book* was written with you, the homemaker, in mind. . . . Whether you're an experienced cook, or a newcomer to the world of cooking three meals a day, we want it to be your best friend in the kitchen." It's signed "The Editors."

Well, bless your heart, Editors. My best friend in the kitchen is my microwave, which heats two of the three meals I eat every day.

While the Editors might have missed a few episodes of *Maude* and probably the entire feminist movement, most of the *BH&GNCB* baking recipes have withstood the test of time.

Here's a tip for this one: if you start to make it and realize you don't quite have enough molasses, make up the difference with honey. I was desperate one morning and tried it—pretty delicious!

This recipe serves 8 to 10, depending on how you slice it.

A T F Gingerbread

YOU'LL NEED

An 8-inch square or 9-inch round baking pan

1 stick (1/2 cup) unsalted butter
2 tablespoons dark brown sugar
1 large egg
1 cup molasses
1 cup dark beer (see Tip)
2 1/4 cups all-purpose flour
1 teaspoon baking soda
1 1/2 teaspoons ground cloves
1 teaspoon ground cinnamon
Dash of salt
1/2 cup crystallized ginger, broken into small chunks (see Wallet Warning)
Gingery Cream Cheese Frosting (optional, page 73)

Tip: That's roughly two-thirds of a bottle from a six-pack. Measure out the 1 cup and drink the rest of the bottle, not the rest of the six-pack. Remember: friends don't let friends bake drunk.

Wallet Warning: Crystallized ginger is expensive. I think 1/2 cup ran me something like $5 at the local Safeway. But the cake was worth the expense. Especially since I had 5 bottles of dark beer left over.

1. Center a rack and preheat the oven to 350 degrees F. Spray the sides and bottom of pan with baking spray.
2. Cream the butter with the mixer on medium speed, add the brown sugar, and beat well.
3. Still at medium speed, add the egg, molasses, and dark beer all together. Beat well for 1 to 2 minutes.
4. In a separate bowl, dry whisk the flour, baking soda, ground cloves, ground cinnamon, and salt together. Add to the batter in thirds, beating well after each addition.
5. Using a spatula, fold in the crystallized ginger (remember our folding lesson with the Swedish Visiting Cake on page 62).
6. Pour the batter into the prepared pan and bake for 45 to 50 minutes, or until a toothpick or thin knife inserted in the center comes out clean.

CONTINUED –

I don't know the real name of this recipe, but it's from my neighbor Jane Marshall. Her mom was a home economics instructor back in the '50s, so consequently, Jane knows a good recipe when she sees one. She jotted this down after watching *Bon Appétit Catering* in July 1985. While Jane's not a big fan of gingerbread, she loves this recipe. I call it ATF (as in the Bureau of Alcohol, Tobacco, Firearms and Explosives) because it's made with dark beer and crystallized ginger. Bite into one of those chunks of crystallized ginger, and you think your mouth might explode. And then you're addicted.

Like our previous gingerbread recipe, this serves 8 to 10, depending on how many come back for seconds.

ATF Gingerbread — CONTINUED

7. Cool the cake in the pan for 10 minutes. Remove the cake from the pan using our plate-over-pan method and flip it onto a cake rack (see page 28). Continue cooling the cake. You can also serve the cake right in the pan, if you so desire.

8. If you decided to go for the frosting, spread it over the cake. Or serve as is. Like with our other gingerbread recipe (page 69), you can make your friends friendlier, or curl up in your La-Z-Boy and eat alone with your cat.

VARIATIONS

This is where using your colleagues as guinea pigs comes in handy. One week, I decided to double the ATF Gingerbread recipe, but instead of doubling the all-purpose flour, I stuck with the original amount and added an equal amount of whole wheat. Reporter Ari Shapiro, who loves to cook and bake, weighed in:

From: Ari Shapiro
To: Melissa Gray
Subject: RE: Today's cake
This is a really awesome cake. I love that it's hardly sweet, and that gingery bite!

From: Melissa Gray
To: Ari Shapiro
Subject: RE: Today's cake
Yeah, that bite would have been a little MORE gingery if I'd had another 1/2 cup of crystallized ginger! Ouch! The flour mix is half white/half wheat. Can you tell the wheat's in there?

From: Ari Shapiro
To: Melissa Gray
Subject: RE: Today's cake
Yeah, the cake feels rustic in a good way. I think it's a combination of several things—the wheat flour, the beer, the amount of sugar . . .

From: Melissa Gray
To: Ari Shapiro
Subject: RE: Today's cake
I'll file this one under "rustic" then! Thanks for the feedback!

From: Ari Shapiro
To: Melissa Gray
Subject: RE: Today's cake
Thanks for the cake!

Gingery Cream Cheese Frosting

Now, as you might suspect, ATF Gingerbread is a more aromatic and less sweet gingerbread than what you're used to. If you're one of those who needs the sweet and doesn't mind just a little more kick, I recommend this frosting, which I found in *Sharing Our Best*, a community cookbook project sponsored by the Gideon Sunday School Class of Providence Baptist Church, in Gloucester, Virginia.

The recipe makes enough to heavily frost one 8- or 9-inch layer, or the top of a cake baked in a 10-inch tube pan.

YOU'LL NEED

3 ounces cream cheese, at room temperature
½ stick (¼ cup) unsalted butter, at room temperature
1 teaspoon vanilla extract
2 cups confectioners' sugar
½ teaspoon ground ginger

Cream the cream cheese, butter, and vanilla at medium speed. Add the confectioners' sugar gradually, add the ginger, and beat until smooth.

Like, baking with chocolate:

A FEW THINGS YOU SHOULD KNOW

If you've never seen the 1993 magical realist Mexican film *Like Water for Chocolate*, run—do not walk—to your nearest DVD rental or access your Netflix account. There's a scene involving a chocolate mole (mo-lay), a sauce that might possibly make you daydream sensual thoughts of seducing your lover by baking with chocolate. Unfortunately for me, my lover/husband hates chocolate. If only I knew how to bake Cheetos.

People who love chocolate REALLY love chocolate, so when you're making a chocolate cake for the office, you're practically guaranteed the status of a minor deity for at least a day. But not all chocolate is the same, and it's important you use the best chocolate for the job.

Chocolate comes from the beans of the cacao tree. The beans are roasted, then crushed to separate the meat, or nib of the bean, from the husk and the germ. Through grinding and heating, the nibs produce chocolate liquor, which is about 55 percent cocoa butter. The liquor is then processed into different types of chocolate.

Unsweetened chocolate, also known as baking chocolate, smells great but tastes terrible. It usually comes in 1 inch squares.

Bittersweet or semisweet chocolate can be maddening, because there's no set rule for how much sugar can be added to the chocolate, and each manufacturer has its own "secret" formula. You may have to try a few brands to find the one that you prefer. Bittersweet and semisweet chocolate are made by combining chocolate liquor, sugar, cocoa butter, lecithin (a soybean product), and vanilla. They're sold in bars, blocks, and morsels.

Most white chocolate isn't really chocolate. It's made from cocoa butter without the chocolate liquor. The cocoa butter is mixed with sugar, milk, and vanilla. It's very rich, has a very low melting point, and shouldn't be substituted for regular chocolate. It's also sold in bars, blocks, and morsels.

Milk chocolate is ideal for cravings, not for baking, so forget that. It's got a higher milk and sugar content than other true chocolates.

Unsweetened cocoa is a powder made by removing at least 75 percent of the cocoa butter from chocolate liquor.

Dutch process unsweetened cocoa is similar to unsweetened cocoa, except the acid in the chocolate has been neutralized before processing. This gives the cocoa a milder flavor and makes it easier to dissolve. It should only be used in recipes where baking powder is the primary leavening agent. Dutch process and regular unsweetened cocoa are NOT interchangeable.

Both cocoas are sold in lidded containers. When baking with them, you will usually mix them with other dry ingredients before adding them to batter (see Like, Baking with Chocolate, Part II on page 175 for more about Dutch process cocoa).

The chocolate you use will depend on how much you want to spend and how discriminating your chocolate tastes are. A good grocery store will have a variety of brands to choose from. One of my co-workers, Julia Redpath Buckley, swears by the Safeway generic brand of chocolate chips. I'm a sucker for Hershey's extra-dark Dutch process unsweetened cocoa. I like Lindt's bittersweet bars, but Ghirardelli also makes a kick-ass chocolate.

Chocolate can keep for years. You'll want to wrap your bars and blocks in aluminum foil and then put them in a zipper-top bag before storing them in a cool, dark place. Why? Because the cocoa butter in chocolate is a whorish sponge, which will pick up the flavor of anything it's standing with. When you unwrap your chocolate for later use, you might notice a white film. It's not the creeping crud, it's that whorish cocoa butter separating from the solids. It's harmless and will disappear when the chocolate is melted. Also keep your cocoa tightly lidded in that same dark, cool place.

Chocolate is sensitive and needs to be treated gently. Never melt your chocolate over direct heat. Use a double boiler or a bowl that fits into a saucepan filled with simmering water, which you maintain over low heat. You can also preheat an oven to 225 degrees F, set your chocolate in a bowl in the oven, then immediately turn off the oven and wait a few minutes. You can also nuke chocolate in the microwave. Start with 30 seconds on high power. Initially, the chocolate won't look much different (it might look like a bar of chocolate in a bowl), so you'll have to use a knife or fork to see if it's melted. It's important not to overheat chocolate. Sensitive, remember. And always break your chocolate chunk into smaller pieces before you try to melt it. Let your melted chocolate cool until it's slightly tepid before adding to other ingredients.

Chocolate Pound Cake

YOU'LL NEED
A 10-inch tube pan

3 cups all-purpose flour
3 cups sugar
½ cup unsweetened cocoa
1 stick (½ cup) unsalted butter, at room temperature
1 cup shortening
1¼ cups milk
½ teaspoon baking powder
½ teaspoon salt
1 teaspoon vanilla extract
5 large eggs

1. Position a rack so the cake will sit in the middle of the oven and preheat the oven to 325 degrees F. Line the bottom of your pan with parchment paper and spray the sides and bottom with baking spray.
2. In the bowl of an electric mixer, dry whisk the flour, sugar, and cocoa together.
3. Gradually add the butter, shortening, and milk and beat on medium speed until smooth.
4. Add the baking powder and salt, and beat until incorporated.
5. Still on medium speed, add the vanilla extract and then add the eggs, one at a time, beating after each addition.

CONTINUED —

Know some chocoholics? If they're not in rehab, they're going to become your very best friends when you bring this baby in. It's another recipe Momma gave me. I made it for the *Morning Edition* overnight staff during the month after the 2000 presidential election, when we were still wondering who'd won: Bush or Gore. At 3 A.M., the cake was on the counter. At 3:16 it was gone. The cake would have lasted until 3:20, but Newscast's Dave Mattingly had five pieces. He said one was for Carl Kasell, but I know that was a lie.

This cake slices thin and can serve between 20 and 32 people.

Chocolate Pound Cake — CONTINUED

6. Pour the batter into the prepared pan and bake for 1½ hours, or until a toothpick or thin knife inserted in the center comes out clean.
7. Cool the cake in the pan for 10 minutes. Remove the cake from the pan using our rack-over-pan method and flip it onto a plate (see page 28). Continue cooling the cake.

Wait, wait, wait Melissa! In the first part of this book we spent God knows how many brain cells going over how to properly cream butter and sugar and add the dry ingredients, and this recipe doesn't follow that standard mixing technique! What gives?

It may have something to do with baker's preference. This recipe will give you a moist, dense cake if you follow the directions as written. I suspect since the baking powder is added later, it has less time to react to the liquid and there is also less beating here (less beating = less air in batter). When I tried the recipe with the standard mixing procedure, I got a lighter, fluffier, and much taller cake, which rose about an inch above the cake pan. A different texture, but the same taste. I prefer it denser, so I go with the original mixing instructions.

If you collect recipes, you're going to come across a lot that don't conform to that standard mixing technique. Always follow directions as intended, then experiment with your technique when you've muscled up your skills.

Mary Carole Battle's Mother's Wacky Cake with Seven-Minute Frosting

CHOCOLATE CAKE WITH LESS FUSS

NEW TECHNIQUE ALERT!

SEPARATING EGGS

YOU'LL NEED

A 9-inch square or round baking pan

1½ cups all-purpose flour
1 cup sugar
½ teaspoon salt
¼ cup unsweetened cocoa
1 teaspoon baking soda
1 teaspoon vanilla extract
1 tablespoon white vinegar
6 tablespoons vegetable oil
1 cup cold water
Seven-Minute Frosting (recipe follows)

1. Center a rack and preheat the oven to 350 degrees F. Spray the sides and bottom of the pan with baking spray.

2. In a large mixing bowl, dry whisk the flour, sugar, salt, cocoa, and baking soda together.

3. Make 3 holes, or "wells," in the dry ingredients. Pour the vanilla extract into one well, the vinegar into a second one, and the oil into the third.

4. Pour the cold water over the mixture, and stir until no longer lumpy. Feel free to use a hand mixer or a pair of Popeye arms (you have been eating your spinach, haven't you?), which you will need soon for the frosting.

CONTINUED –

Speaking of totally different mixing techniques (see the facing page), *All Things Considered* did a series one year, asking listeners about what foods meant summer to them. Mary Carole Battle of St. Petersburg, Florida, wrote in, saying it wasn't summer unless a wacky cake was involved. She told us about celebrating her birthday when she was a kid. It's on August 17, and she would celebrate with a friend who also had a birthday around that time. The friend's mother would put a fancy, store-bought cake in front of her daughter, and Mary Carole's mother would put a wacky cake in front of Mary Carole.

Michele Norris interviewed Mary Carole to find out how to make the cake, which involves no butter, no eggs, and no milk. In fact, the Seven-Minute Frosting takes more time to make than the cake!

After the story aired, we were bombarded by more listener e-mail. People wrote in about their wacky cakes, which were called crazy cakes, Joe cakes, and WW II cakes. We were told that this cake, with its dearth of dairy products, was a desperate homemaker's answer to wartime shortages. Regardless of its real name and origin, it's a fun and easy cake to do, especially with a competent seven-year-old. And it tastes pretty good!

This cake will serve about 8 to 10, depending on how you slice it.

Mary Carole Battle's Mother's Wacky Cake with Seven-Minute Frosting — CONTINUED

5. Pour the batter into the pan and bake for 30 to 35 minutes, or until a toothpick or thin knife inserted in the center comes out clean.
6. Cool the cake in the pan for 10 minutes. Remove the cake from the pan using our plate-over-pan method and flip it onto a cake rack (see page 28). Continue cooling the cake and frost it. Or simply frost the top of the cake and serve in the pan for even less fuss.

Seven-Minute Frosting

This makes enough frosting to heavily ice a 9-inch cake, or the top of a cake baked in a 10-inch tube pan.

YOU'LL NEED

A double boiler, real or improvised (see step 2)
A hand-held electric mixer OR somebody with Popeye arms

2 large eggs, at room temperature
1½ cups sugar
¼ teaspoon cream of tartar
⅓ cup cold water
1 teaspoon vanilla extract

1. Separate the eggs.
2. Mix the egg whites, sugar, cream of tartar, and cold water in the top part of a double boiler, OR in the top of an improvised double boiler: Use a heat-proof bowl that will fit over a pan with about 2 inches of water in it, or a small saucepan that will sit inside of a larger one containing water. Using a hand mixer or Popeye arms, beat the mixture for about 1 minute.
3. Place the top over the bottom half of the double boiler (or place the heat-proof bowl into the pan of water). Bring the water to a gentle boil, and beat the mixture on high speed for 7 minutes, or until you have soft peaks (see page 106).
4. Remove from the heat and add the vanilla. Beat for 1 or 2 minutes more.
5. Cool slightly, then frost away!

NEW TECHNIQUE

SEPARATING EGGS

Oh, there are fancy gadgets out there for separating eggs, and not-so-fancy gadgets, and then there's the method where you carefully crack your shell in half and use the bottom part to catch the yolk. I use the most stripped-down method of all: my clean, dry, bare hands. It's amazing how well this works, though it grosses out a competent seven-year-old. It also grosses out some adults. It's a good party trick to have in your repertoire, trust me.

Have 3 bowls ready: one bowl to catch the individual egg white, one to hold your collection of egg whites, and one for the yolks. Crack an egg against the edge of a bowl, then dump the egg into a cupped hand, catching the yolk and letting the white slip through your fingers into the empty bowl. Then gently slide the egg yolk into the yolk bowl. Next, transfer the egg white into the third bowl: the egg white collection bowl.

Why use a designated bowl for the egg you're separating? Because it's crucial NOT to get any yolk mixed in with the egg whites. Suppose you use only two bowls and you've separated eight eggs and are about to separate the ninth, only to realize you've broken the yolk and it's now seeping into the collection of egg whites—ACK! You are so screwed. Unless you like really big omelets. But this book is about cakes, not omelets. And egg whites with yolk in them are not going to whip into soft or stiff peaks, and one of those is the stage you need to get them to.

Hmmm. But what to do with all those yolks? Well, there are cakes that are yolk-heavy (Lord Baltimore, page 189), and there are frostings that are also yolk heavy (Lane Cake Filling and Frosting, page 193). Rather than toss my yolks, I freeze them for later use in cakes and frostings. I sprinkle a bit of water over them, and add either a dash of salt or sugar as a preservative. Since I bake on Sundays, I'll move my frozen yolks to the refrigerator to thaw Friday night, then leave them out for 1 or 2 hours before using them on Sunday.

So many yolks, so few punch lines.

Cocoa Bread with Stewed Yard Peaches

YOU'LL NEED

An 8-inch square or 9-inch round baking pan

FOR THE COCOA BREAD

1 stick (½ cup) unsalted butter
1 cup boiling water
½ cup molasses
½ cup sugar
2 large eggs, lightly beaten
2 cups self-rising flour (see Tip)
½ teaspoon baking soda
¼ cup unsweetened cocoa
1 teaspoon ground cinnamon

FOR THE STEWED PEACHES

6 cups sliced peeled peaches (see Tip)
¾ cup sugar
½ cup water

Tips: Do NOT use all-purpose flour without compensating for the substitution—remember your briefing at the beginning of this book (page 34)! If you don't have self-rising, add 3 teaspoons of baking powder and 1 teaspoon of salt to 2 cups of all-purpose flour, and you should be fine.

If you don't have fresh peaches, frozen are best. Use two 16-ounce bags. But you can also use canned peaches, so long as you drain the syrup off.

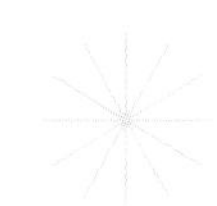

TO MAKE THE COCOA BREAD

1. Center a rack and preheat the oven to 350 degrees F. Spray the sides and bottom of your pan with baking spray.
2. On the stove top or in the microwave, melt the butter and set aside to cool.
3. Boil some water and measure out 1 cup.
4. In a large bowl, whisk together the boiling water, melted butter, molasses, and sugar. Let cool, then whisk in the eggs.
5. In a separate bowl, dry whisk the flour, baking soda, unsweetened cocoa, and cinnamon together.
6. Add a third of the flour mixture to the molasses mixture and whisk until smooth. Repeat until all of the flour mixture is blended in.
7. Pour the batter into the prepared pan and bake for 30 minutes, or until a toothpick or thin knife inserted in the middle comes out clean. While the cake is baking, stew the peaches.

TO MAKE THE STEWED PEACHES

8. Bring the peaches, sugar, and water to a boil in a medium saucepan over medium heat, stirring gently until the sugar dissolves.

9. Reduce the heat to low and simmer for 10 minutes.

TO SERVE

10. Cool the bread in the pan for 10 minutes, then unmold onto a serving plate and serve warm with the stewed peaches. This can be tricky in the office. I usually wrap the bread in parchment paper and aluminum foil. At work I remove the foil, wrap the cake with dampened paper towels, and microwave at low power to warm it up. If you can't do that, don't worry: it's good cool, too. You can serve the peaches hot, cold, or at room temperature, depending on your fancy (I like them a little cooler than the cake, but they're good hot, too).

Another great find for me has been *Southern Living* magazine's annual recipe books. They're a little skimpy on the cake recipes, but the ones they do have are something good. This recipe (pictured on page 40), from the 2005 edition, doesn't require a lot of beating, so you can go low-tech and mix it by hand.

Cocoa bread was a welcome change when my co-workers were getting a little sick of gingerbread. But here's the thing: If you bring it to work, you have to bring the stewed peaches in a separate container, and leave directions next to the cocoa bread. Otherwise, instead of eating the bread and peaches together, they'll eat each of them alone. Double the recipe if you want more than 8 servings.

Chapter Two

BRING ME BUNDTS AND BRING ME MORE SPICE AND VICE!

HOW TO BAKE A DROP-DEAD GORGEOUS CAKE WITH HARDLY ANY EFFORT. PLUS SPICE, FRUIT, AND DRUNKEN CAKES—SO VERY, VERY NICE!

GIMME THEM PURDY CAKES!

A brief history of the Bundt pan

Here's the thing about a good Bundt pan:

It can turn the most pedestrian of cakes into a real glamour-puss. That brown sugar cake back on page 42? It looks all homey-Americana when done in a regular ol' tube pan. But when I pour that batter into my Nordic Ware Bavaria Bundt Pan then bake, cool, and dust with confectioners' sugar, *wunderbar*, baby! It's GORGEOUS!

I say *wunderbar* instead of *voilà* because the Bundt pan has Germanic roots. Over in Deutschland, it's known as a *kugelhopf*, because that's what they use to bake *kugelhopf*, a breadlike cake with seedless raisins. *Kugelhopf* literally means "risen ball," which tells of its doughy, yeasty origins.

Kugelhopf pans are circular, deep, and fluted. They were traditionally made from enameled pottery or heavy cast iron, which means you'd need a pair of Popeye arms to even use one. That changed in 1950, when H. David Dalquist responded to a friend's request. He was the founder of Nordic Ware Corporation. She was president of the Minneapolis chapter of the Hadassah Society. The members of this Jewish women's organization wanted to make kugelhopf, which is also known as *bundkuchen*, meaning "a gathering cake." They needed nice pans that were easy to use. Dalquist modified some existing Scandinavian designs to create a new pan out of lightweight aluminum. To distinguish his creation from the Bund, a pro-Hitler German-American group from the 1930s, Dalquist added the letter "t" to "bund," and *voilà!* or *wunderbar!* or ta-dah! The Bundt pan was born! Dalquist also pioneered the glass carousel that rotates in microwaves, but that's another story.

The year 1966 was when the Bundt pan really took off, thanks to the ingenuity of one Ella Rita Helfrich. The Houston, Texas, housewife won second prize in the Pillsbury Bake-Off Contest that year with a cake EVERYBODY simply HAD to try: Tunnel of Fudge Cake. And they had to have a Bundt pan to try it in. And yes, you're going to get your shot at it, too, but let me finish my story.

If you visit Minnesota, you can tour the Nordic Ware factory and you might be able to get a discounted pan when you do. In most stores, they cost anywhere from $25 to $50, depending on size and design. Our host Michele Norris has a sister named Cindy who lives in Minnesota, and Cindy sometimes supplies me with a surprise pan, which of course means *All Things Considered* gets a Bundt cake the next Monday. I cruise the cookware section of discount stores for my other pans, most of which I've bought for less than $16. I've now got seven total, including the Cathedral, which makes us feel like we're eating a mini–Notre Dame. But you can also get a pan shaped like a star, fleur-de-lis, or a ring of Christmas trees, if you so desire.

Because of the intricacies of some Bundt molds, you've got to really work it with your floured baking spray. I do not recommend baking a stratified coffee cake in a Bundt, and I'd be careful baking any recipes that include fruit, due to the headache generated when trying to unmold those cakes from anything more intricate than the traditional, fluted Bundt pan. Don't forget when you use a Bundt pan, the top of the cake bakes in the bottom of the pan. If the cake "domes" during baking and is quite high, you'll need to use a serrated bread knife to even it up before you flip it onto a cooling rack or a serving plate. You don't need frosting; leave that for sheet cakes and layer cakes. Visually, Bundt cakes are meant to stand on their own, though you can highlight their design and taste with a dusting of sugar or drizzle of glaze.

Tunnel of Fudge Cake

YOU'LL NEED

A 12-cup Bundt or 10-inch tube pan

FOR THE CAKE

3½ sticks (1¾ cups) unsalted butter, at room temperature

1¾ cups sugar

6 large eggs

2 cups confectioners' sugar

2¼ cups all-purpose flour

¾ cup unsweetened cocoa (IMPORTANT: NOT DUTCH PROCESS!)

2 cups chopped walnuts

FOR THE GLAZE

¾ cup confectioners' sugar

¼ cup unsweetened cocoa

4 to 6 teaspoons milk

CONTINUED —

OK, here is the recipe that won Ella Rita Helfrich $5,000 in 1966. (FYI—that's about $30,000 today!) Mrs. Helfrich's ingenuity involved a Pillsbury powdered icing that, when added to the batter, produced a gooey pudding center.

Scientifically, it's a mess, according to Shirley O. Corriher, author of *BakeWise: The Hows and Whys of Successful Baking*. With a background in biochemistry, Shirley's the go-to gal for chefs and bakers with messed-up recipes. According to her, Tunnel of Fudge Cake deliberately has too much sugar. Excess sugar, you see, binds to flour proteins and prevents them from building structure, hence the inside goo. But what about that crisp, crunchy edge? Well, almost any batter will develop a crust if it reaches a high enough temperature. Hard on the outside, liquid chocolate on the inside: that's the magic of the Tunnel of Fudge.

Oh, but for some reason known only to them, Pillsbury took the powdered icing off the market not long after Tunnel of Fudge Cake made its debut. Fortunately, the cake had some vocal supporters. They complained so much that Pillsbury's test kitchen deconstructed the mix. Turns out, it was nothing but confectioners' sugar and cocoa—simple enough!

Now, I've come across several recipes warning, under pain of death, NOT to scrimp on the nuts, that the recipe will simply NOT work and the Four Horsemen of the Apocalypse will show up at your doorstep if you nix the nuts. This is not true. I've made it without the nuts and it comes out just fine. Shirley O. Corriher, our biochemistry baker, did use nuts, but she roasted them to bring out more flavor. She says this improves on the original recipe. You do whatever you darn well please.

Tunnel of Fudge lends itself to big slices, so plan on about 16 servings.

Tunnel of Fudge **Cake** — CONTINUED

TO MAKE THE CAKE

1. Center a rack and preheat the oven to 350 degrees F. Prepare the pan. (See page 21 if you've forgotten how!)
2. Cream the butter on medium speed and gradually add the 1¾ cups of regular sugar (NOT the confectioners'), beating until light and fluffy.
3. Add the eggs, one at a time, beating well after each addition.
4. Gradually add the confectioners' sugar, beating to blend well.
5. Grab a wooden spoon and flex those arms! By hand, stir in the flour and cocoa until well blended. Stir in the nuts.
6. Pour the batter into the prepared pan, spreading it evenly with the spatula.
7. Bake for 45 to 50 minutes, or until the top is set and the edges are beginning to pull away from the sides of the pan. Remember, this cake has a gooey center, so your clean toothpick/skewer/clean knife method will not work!
8. Allow the cake to cool in the pan for 1 hour and 30 minutes. Yes, 1 hour and 30 minutes.
9. This is not a particularly strong cake, so our usual flipping it over to a plate and then to a rack would stress it out. SO: flip directly onto a serving plate and unmold. Allow to cool to room temperature, which will take approximately 2 hours.

TO MAKE THE GLAZE

10. While you're waiting for the Tunnel of Fudge to cool, use your time wisely and mix your glaze: Combine the confectioners' sugar, unsweetened cocoa, and 4 teaspoons of the milk. Beat with a mixer or stir aggressively until the glaze has a smooth texture. Add more teaspoons of milk in order to get it to the right consistency for drizzling.

TO FINISH THE CAKE

11. When the Tunnel of Fudge Cake has reached room temperature, gently spoon the glaze over the top of the cake, allowing some to roll down the sides. Serve.

Butter Rum Cake

YOU'LL NEED

A 12-cup Bundt or 10-inch tube pan

FOR THE CAKE

2 sticks (1 cup) unsalted butter, at room temperature
1 cup sugar
1 cup light brown sugar
4 large eggs
1 tablespoon light rum
3 cups cake flour
1 teaspoon salt
1 teaspoon baking powder
½ teaspoon baking soda
1 cup sour milk (see Tip)

FOR THE GLAZE

⅓ cup unsalted butter
¾ cup sugar
3 tablespoons water
2 teaspoons light rum

Tip: No sour milk? Substitute buttermilk. What? No buttermilk? Add 1 tablespoon of lemon juice or distilled white vinegar to 1 cup of milk and let stand for 5 minutes.

TO MAKE THE CAKE

1. Center a rack and preheat the oven to 325 degrees F. Prepare a Bundt or tube pan.
2. Cream the butter with the mixer on medium speed, and gradually add the sugars, beating well.
3. Add the eggs, one at a time, beating well after each addition.
4. Add the rum and beat to incorporate.
5. In a separate bowl, dry whisk the flour, salt, baking powder, and baking soda together.
6. With the mixer on low, add 1 cup of the flour mixture, beat, and then add ⅓ cup of the sour milk and beat again. Repeat until all of the flour mixture and sour milk are blended into the batter.
7. Increase the mixer speed to medium-high. Beat until all the ingredients are well incorporated.
8. Pour the batter into the pan and bake for 1 hour, or until a toothpick or thin knife inserted in the middle comes out clean.

CONTINUED —

The cake I most associate with a Bundt pan is my Aunt Janet Gray's Rum Cake. The only problem is that it violates my basic tenet of "bake no cake mixes," so off to the Internet I went in search of a from-scratch rum cake.

Unfortunately, I found a LOT of recipes that start with a cake mix, and it took a while for me to track down one that didn't. I'm not sure where I found this recipe (I wasn't planning on writing a book when I jotted it down). But I do know that it originally called for rum extract, and I instead used Bacardi rum, because why use extract when you've got the real deal? It's a winner AND looks FABU in a Bundt.

Note that this recipe calls for cake flour, rather than all-purpose. It will work with all-purpose; it just won't be as light and delicate.

Butter Rum Cake is easily sliced thin, so you can expect to serve 16 to 32.

Butter Rum Cake — CONTINUED

TO MAKE THE GLAZE

9. Melt the butter in a small saucepan over medium heat. Add the sugar, water, and rum and stir until smooth. Remove from the heat.

TO FINISH THE CAKE

10. As soon as the cake is out of the oven, before removing it from the pan, take a toothpick or skewer and poke holes through it. Then pour three-quarters of the glaze over the top of the cake. Let cool in the pan for 10 to 15 minutes.

11. Unmold the cake onto a cake rack and let cool for 10 more minutes. Put a plate under the rack and drizzle the rest of the glaze over the cake.

12. Once the cake has cooled, transfer it to a serving plate—or, hey, how about moving it to your cake carry? It's a lot easier to tote to your office goats that way,

The Naughty Senator PEPPERMINT AND CHOCOLATE RUM MARBLE CAKE

NEW TECHNIQUE ALERT!
MARBLING

YOU'LL NEED

A 12-cup Bundt or 10-inch tube pan
Extra mixing bowl

2 cups sugar
¼ cup unsweetened cocoa
2 sticks (1 cup) unsalted butter, at room temperature
4 large eggs
3½ cups sifted cake flour
3 teaspoons baking powder
½ teaspoon salt
1 cup milk
2 teaspoons peppermint flavoring or extract
½ teaspoon green food coloring
2 teaspoons rum or rum extract

CONTINUED →

I can't believe I'm going to tell this about a cake, but here goes: One summer, a married senator got in trouble in the men's bathroom at a Minneapolis airport. They say Larry Craig was looking for love in all the wrong places. He pleaded guilty to a charge amounting to disturbing the peace. Then, when the story hit cable news, he adamantly stated, repeatedly, that he was "not gay." Oddly, this sex scandal followed another in which a Louisiana senator's phone number was found in the records of an "escort" service, and he'd had to stand up before the cameras and apologize for his behavior. Both men were the family values sort. It's funny; the family values sorts never seem to understand it's not just the questionable behavior that upsets people, it's the hypocrisy. Senator Craig had been on *Meet the Press* during the Monica Lewinsky scandal, and said repeatedly that then president Bill Clinton was a "bad boy, a naughty boy." Naturally, that "bad, naughty boy" rock was thrown through Craig's glass house when his arrest in Minneapolis went public. This whole thing was playing out on TV while I was trying to figure out a good combination of flavors for a marble cake, so the idea of a naughty senator cake was spinning around in my head when I came up with this recipe.

I settled on peppermint, chocolate, and rum. Peppermint, because the senators and congresspeople I've met over the years at NPR always seem to smell of mint. It's a public speaking thing: You don't want to bowl over Robert Siegel with bad breath, though Robert's far too gentlemanly to let you know he's noticed—he's all about the interview. Chocolate, because it's rich and so are most senators. Rum, because, well, rum means debauchery to me. Or at least a sizable impairment of good judgment. That's a story for another book. Anyway . . .

This cake is light and fluffy. It also tastes a little like Junior Mints, and folks are intrigued by the idea of green cake.

The Naughty Senator also lends itself to thin slices and will serve 16 to 32 people, depending on how you slice it (boy, that joke never gets old, does it?).

The Naughty Senator — CONTINUED

1. Center a rack and preheat the oven to 350 degrees F. Prepare the pan.
2. In a small bowl, combine ½ cup of the sugar and all the cocoa. Set aside.
3. With the mixer, cream the butter at medium speed, gradually adding the remaining 1½ cups of sugar. Add the eggs, one at a time, beating well after each addition.
4. In a separate bowl, dry whisk the flour, baking powder, and salt together.
5. With the mixer on low speed, add 1 cup of the flour mixture, beat, then add ⅓ cup of the milk and beat again. Repeat until all of the flour mixture and milk are blended into batter. Beat on medium-high speed for 2 to 3 minutes.
6. Pour half of the batter into a clean medium bowl.
7. Add the peppermint flavoring and a couple of drops of green food coloring to one bowl of batter. NOTE: don't use too much food coloring, just enough to get it a pastel green. Mix well.
8. Pour two-thirds of the now green batter into the bottom of the cake pan. Set aside the remaining green batter.
9. Clean off your mixer beaters, dry, and return them to the mixer.
10. Add the cocoa and sugar mixture to the yellow batter and add the rum or rum extract. Beat until smooth.
11. Using your spatula, pour the chocolate-flavored batter over the green batter in the cake pan.
12. Layer the remaining third of green batter over the chocolate batter. Then marble.

NEW TECHNIQUE

MARBLING

OK, remember the basics of folding from our Swedish Visiting Cake on page 62? You're going to lightly fold your batter *in the pan* in order to get that marble effect, but you're not going to fully fold the ingredients together. Here's how:

Take a small spatula or plastic knife and cut through the middle of the batter ring to the bottom of the pan. Bring the spatula or plastic knife toward you and then up toward the side of the pan. Rotate the cake pan with your other hand and repeat. You'll do 2 rotations total. No more.

13. Bake for 1 hour. When the cake tests done, cool for 15 to 30 minutes in the pan, then unmold onto a cake rack.

VARIATIONS

For a different flavor combination, you can keep half of the batter chocolate, without the rum, and flavor the other half with 1 teaspoon of vanilla extract OR 1 teaspoon of almond extract OR 1 teaspoon of cherry extract, instead of the peppermint.

Oh, but you WANT more rum? Grab that recipe for butter rum glaze on page 91, mix, and drizzle away.

Paula Deen's Almond Sour Cream Pound Cake

YOU'LL NEED

A 12-cup Bundt or 10-inch tube pan

1 cup sliced almonds
2 sticks (1 cup) unsalted butter, at room temperature
3 cups sugar
1 cup sour cream
3 cups all-purpose flour
½ teaspoon baking soda
6 large eggs
½ teaspoon orange extract
½ teaspoon almond extract

1. Center a rack and preheat the oven to 325 degrees F. Prepare the pan.
2. While the oven is preheating, spread out the almonds in a shallow baking pan and toast for 3 minutes. Remove from the oven, toss the almonds in the pan, then return to the oven for 3 more minutes.
3. Cream the butter with the mixer on medium speed and gradually add the sugar. Add the sour cream and beat until smooth.
4. In a separate bowl, dry whisk the flour and baking soda together.
5. Add ½ cup of the flour mixture to the creamed mixture and beat until blended. Add 1 egg, then beat until blended. Repeat until all of the flour mixture and eggs are mixed in.
6. Add the orange extract and almond extract and beat until blended into the batter.
7. Using a wooden spoon or spatula, fold in the toasted almonds.
8. Pour the batter into the prepared pan and bake for 1 hour and 20 minutes, or until the cake tests done.
9. Cool the cake in the pan for 10 minutes. If it's in a decorative Bundt pan and has a domed top (which will be the bottom of the cake), use a long serrated knife to level it. Unmold and allow to cool completely on a cake rack.
10. Dust lightly with confectioners' sugar.

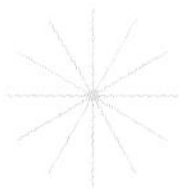

Paula Deen puts my husband's salivary glands into overdrive. He loves her madly. She's old enough to be his momma, but he does not care. She's a Southern cook, an unapologetic Ms. Butter-and-Cream who says, "If you want low-fat fare, get out of my kitchen." But you'd stay put because she's so down-to-earth on her cooking shows. Jimmy and I like to add running commentary: "Here comes the butter!" "I bet she uses shortening next." "She's about to lick that whipped cream right off her fingers!" "There goes a scrap for the dog!"

Paula has one of those rags-to-riches stories: Both parents died by the time she was twenty-three, she married young, then divorced young. To support herself and her kids, she started a catering business, selling bag lunches to workers in Savannah. She opened her first restaurant there, the Lady and Sons, in 1996, then self-published her first cookbooks. By 2002, she had her own cooking show on the Food Network, *Paula's Home Cooking*.

I first heard of Paula Deen in 2003, shortly after Jimmy and I married. He was downstairs watching TV, homesick for Deep Southern cooking. Then Paula's show came on. "Oh my god! She's using PIG!" he cried. He became progressively more homesick as he watched Paula fry up bacon and then stir up corn bread in a skillet. Paula Deen's show became a regular event in our house until Jimmy got somewhat used to living in the DC 'burbs.

The last time Jimmy, his dad, his brother, and I were in Savannah, we tried to get a meal from the Lady and Sons, but the line was so long, we ended up eating at a Scottish pub down the street. This caused my father-in-law mild distress as he wasn't used to men in "skirts." I don't think we'll be getting him into a tartan anytime soon. But we will get him and his sons to Paula's restaurant one of these days.

This recipe comes from Paula's show *Paula Deen's Wedding*. She says this cake is to be baked in a tube pan and frosted with almond buttercream, and then there's a mysterious note that says this recipe would have to be modified to make it into a wedding cake. How, it does not explain. But as far as I'm concerned, if it's good enough for a wedding cake, it's good enough for the *All Things Considered* staff. Some days I feel like I'm married to all of them anyway, so what the heck.

The cake was so good that I never got around to making the buttercream frosting. I now make it in a decorative Bundt pan, with an added cup of chopped toasted almonds, and I dust the cooled cake with confectioners' sugar.

You'll notice that Paula's mixing directions differ from the usual method of beating the eggs into the creamed butter and sugar and then adding the dry and wet ingredients, and finally the flavorings. She also doesn't call for salt, so no, that's not a typo!

If you want to try it with buttercream, turn to page 168 for an easy buttercream recipe. Just nix the honey and add 1 teaspoon of almond extract.

And yes, this cake can be sliced thin, so expect to serve anywhere from 16 to 32 people (all together now) "depending on how you slice it."

Coffee Spice Cake

YOU'LL NEED

A 12-cup Bundt or 10-inch tube pan

3/4 cup cold strong coffee
3/4 cup shortening
1 1/2 cups dark brown sugar
1/4 cup molasses
3 large eggs
2 1/2 cups cake flour
3 teaspoons baking powder
1/4 teaspoon baking soda
1/4 teaspoon salt
1/4 teaspoon ground ginger
1 1/2 teaspoons ground cinnamon
1/4 teaspoon ground cloves
1/4 teaspoon ground nutmeg

1. Obtain coffee. This is the dark roasted stuff, not watered-down diner coffee. Brew it yourself, or use this as an excuse to run down to your local coffee shop and treat yourself to a grande mocha Frappuccino or a chai latte because you simply haven't had enough go-go juice today and would like to spend the next few hours bouncing off the walls of your kitchen.

   (Actually, I use this recipe as an excuse to get a pedicure. The shop is located next door to my local Starbucks. I think a full pedicure costs roughly the same as a grande mocha Frappuccino and lasts at least twice as long.)

2. Center a rack and preheat the oven to 350 degrees F. Prepare the cake pan.

3. Cream the shortening with the mixer on medium speed, and add the brown sugar gradually. Increase the mixer speed to medium-high and beat until fluffy, roughly 3 minutes.

4. Shift the mixer to low speed. Add the molasses, then the eggs, one at a time, beating well after each addition.

5. In a separate bowl, dry whisk the flour, baking powder, baking soda, salt, and spices together.

6. Add a third of the flour mixture to the creamed mixture, beat, then add 1/4 cup of the coffee and beat on medium until well blended. Repeat 2 more times.

7. Pour the batter into the pan and bake for 45 minutes, or until the cake tests done.

8. Cool for 10 to 15 minutes in the pan, unmold onto a cake rack, and cool completely.

9. Sprinkle with coarse sugar or dust with confectioners' sugar.

VARIATION

Less Spice, More Mocha Coffee Spice Cake

Even though the original recipe got the official "mmm, mmm, good cake!" designation from the staff, I decided it was just a little too close to gingerbread and not close enough to coffee, or at least grande mocha Frappuccino. I did want a dash of barista added to this baby, I have to admit. So, I decided to re-cake. The addition of chocolate was generally welcomed by all.

CONTINUED –

This isn't a traditional coffee cake—it's a cake in which cold coffee is an ingredient. It seems a lot of older recipes used coffee in cakes, and I'm kind of surprised that Starbucks hasn't capitalized on this, what with America's newly developed love of all things java.

To me, this cake is reminiscent of gingerbread, but the office foodies say it has a more complex taste, thanks to the coffee, cloves, nutmeg, and cinnamon, in addition to the ginger, molasses, and brown sugar. The cake flour gives it a light and very delicate crumb. I bake it in a Bundt pan and sprinkle coarse sugar over it (see picture on page 84) because it reminds me of Christmas ginger cookies. But you can also dust it with confectioners' sugar.

This cake has a more delicate crumb and doesn't slice thinly, so it will serve anywhere from 16 to 24 people.

Coffee Spice Cake – CONTINUED

FOR THE CHOCOLATE DRIZZLE (SEE TIP)

YOU'LL NEED

Two 1-ounce squares unsweetened chocolate
1½ cups (about 1 small can) sweetened condensed milk
2 tablespoons cold strong coffee

Tip: Here's where the essence of mocha Frappuccino comes in.

TO REMAKE THE CAKE

1. In hopes of getting a richer, moister crumb, I ditched the ¾ cup of shortening and used 1½ sticks (¾ cup) of unsalted butter instead. This did make the crumb moister, but it was still rather delicate. I also ditched the ginger completely. Because I wanted to do a chocolate drizzle on the cake, I opted to use a Bundt pan that has a lot of vertical ridges in it: vertical ridges = more places for the chocolate to run into and stick.

   Follow the main recipe to bake and cool the cake, making the above adjustments.

2. In the top of a double boiler (or an improvised one), melt the unsweetened chocolate over water at a medium boil until smooth.
3. Add the sweetened condensed milk. Stir until fully incorporated, and continue stirring for about 5 minutes, until the mixture has thickened. Then add the coffee.
4. Remove from the heat and stir occasionally until it's time to drizzle over the cooled cake.
5. Use a teaspoon or a soup spoon and let your inner Jackson Pollock take over to the extent that your inner Martha Stewart doesn't freak out about the kitchen mess. If the drizzle has solizzled (that's Snoop Dogg for "solidified"), just get a medium boil going again and stir until the mixture is smooth.

Office CAKE LORE

Jonathan "Smokey" Baer has been with *All Things Considered* for thirty years. Some might say he's eaten his way through thirty years of *ATC*, such is his reputation as an office grazer. Every office has one or two: wherever there's food, there they are. Yet, Smokey is remarkably fit, younger looking than his fifty-plus years. And he has a discriminating palate.

"This cake is not one of your best cakes" he'll tell me on his first bite. "I'm not saying it's bad, just that it's not one of your best." He chews, "the crumb is a little too dry"; he swallows, "and I hate nuts"; he cuts another slice, "but I can see how some people might like this cake"; he licks his fingers, "nice frosting, though."

Thanks, Smokes! I know you critique with love.

As much as he likes to eat, he also likes to bake, which is how I roped Smokey into making a cake for the staff when I was on vacation.

There I was, enjoying myself in sunny Florida when my BlackBerry started buzzing. I got not one, not two, not three, but four e-mails from colleagues about the event we all now refer to as Smokey's Tragedy. He had baked the Coffee Spice Cake (it's his favorite), and happily brought it in to share (Good boy, Smokey), but as he was holding his cake carry aloft at his cubicle, trying to unsnap it to get to the cake, the entire bottom, cake and all, tumbled to the floor. "It had a little more fiber in it," he told me later, grinning, "*carpet* fiber." Apparently most of the staff followed the five-second rule and passed on partaking, but not Smokey: "It was ugly, but it was still very, very good," he noted later, with a Cheshire cat-like grin.

Hey, Lady— NICE RACK!

THINGS YOU MIGHT LIKE TO KNOW ABOUT WHAT MAKES LITTLE GIRLS SO NICE

I hate it when someone asks me a question and I don't know the answer. Like when I've made a cake and I'm telling someone what's in it and he says "Mace? What's mace? Where do you get that?" And I answer, "From my spice rack."

While that's TRUE, it's not the right answer. I work at NPR, where, if we don't know the right answer, we Google. And then we confirm with librarian Mary Glendenning, because the LAST thing we want to get is a picky ol' listener letter telling us how very WRONG we were and how the listener expected OH SO MUCH BETTER FROM US. Truly, some of them try to guilt-trip us over innocent boo-boos, like the time I mistook Zsa Zsa Gabor for her sister Eva. It's not just the high exalted mission of journalists to get every miniscule detail absolutely correct; it's a point of pride and self-preservation. And so when someone gets it wrong at NPR, there's a twenty-four-hour group shunning, and our editors make the offending party wear a sign with "slattern" scrawled across it. Those of us who read *Jane Eyre* know what that means.

I want to spare you such indignity. Hopefully, your workplace isn't so creatively Victorian. But if it is, here are the basics about the origins of spices. If you need more details, do like the NPR staff do—GOOGLE!

Ginger is ground from a plant that's grown in China and India. It's pungent and aromatic and when ground is generally light bone to orangey-tan colored. More details about ginger back on page 68.

Nutmeg is ground from the seed of a tree native to Southeast Asia. It's strongly aromatic, with a little hint of citrus and pine. It's generally light brown.

Mace is kind of cool. It is ground from the lacey little red covering that grows OVER the seed from which nutmeg is ground. It tastes like nutmeg, but it's more delicate. Its color is generally deep brick orange.

Cloves come either whole or ground. They're the nail-shaped, unopened bud of a tree that grows in Indonesia, Zanzibar, and Madagascar. Ground cloves are an orangey brown, and taste strong, sweet, and almost hot.

As for cinnamon, well, this is a shocker: A lot of what we call cinnamon is actually from the cassia tree, and that cinnamon is often referred to as bastard cinnamon. True cinnamon is the thin, inner bark of the *Cinnamomum verum* tree, which grows in Sri Lanka. The bark is stripped off and dried in the sun, where it curls into those little scrolls, cinnamon sticks, that are sometimes served with hot chocolate or coffee around the holidays. Bastard cinnamon is harvested the same way, but cinnamon scrolls from the cassia tree are harder to grind by hand. True cinnamon has a sweeter and more refined taste than bastard cinnamon, but essentially it is the same flavor. Cassia may be a bastard, but it is related to *Cinnamomum verum*. Kind of like Patty Duke and her identical cousin (oh, Google that if you don't know the reference). You can get cinnamon in scrolls or ground; either way, it's reddish brown in color.

Spanish Meringue Cake

NEW TECHNIQUE ALERT!

BEATING EGG WHITES

YOU'LL NEED

A 9-inch springform pan
The whisk attachment for your mixer

FOR THE CAKE

½ teaspoon baking soda
1 cup buttermilk
1 stick (½ cup) unsalted butter, at room temperature
1¼ cups light brown sugar
2¼ cups cake flour
1 teaspoon baking powder
½ teaspoon ground cinnamon
¼ teaspoon ground nutmeg
1 large egg
3 large egg yolks
1 teaspoon vanilla extract
1 cup walnuts, chopped

FOR THE MERINGUE

3 large egg whites (see Tips)
⅛ teaspoon cream of tartar
¾ cup light brown sugar
½ teaspoon ground cinnamon
¼ teaspoon ground nutmeg

Tips: You're making meringue, which means you're whipping the living bejesus out of egg whites. It is crucial to your operations that your eggs be ROOM TEMPERATURE and that your whisk and mixing bowl be clean and perfectly dry.

Notice you need 3 egg yolks for the cake and 3 egg whites for the meringue. So you'll need to separate 3 eggs. Use 3 bowls and your clean, dry hands (see instructions on page 81) OR a fancy-pants egg separator to do this.

1. Because of the meringue topping, your usual "center a rack" does not apply. You'll want to position the rack in the lower third of your oven and preheat to 325 degrees F.

TO MAKE THE CAKE

2. Prepare your springform pan. You'll want to use a springform because it's easier to "unmold" the cake without messing up the meringue topping.

3. In a small bowl, stir the baking soda into the buttermilk and set aside.

CONTINUED –

All the cakes in this book are great cakes (why would I write a book about cakes and give you bad recipes?), but THIS cake is one of my top ten. It's from Carole Walter's award-winning book *Great Cakes*, but it's not her cake. It's her version of a cake by one Robert McNamara of Atlantic City, New Jersey, baked for a contest in 1975. But it wasn't his recipe, either. It was his mother's.

According to Carole, the original cake had "a lightly spiced brown sugar base that was topped with chopped walnuts, then covered with a brown sugar meringue. When baked, the meringue turned into a delicate, chewy caramel-flavored topping." Her recipe has a light, moist crumb, and with all the spices and the meringue, it goes really well with coffee.

A note about the directions: comedian Phil Hartman used to do a skit on *Saturday Night Live* called "The Anal-Retentive Fisherman." The character seemed like he'd never get around to actually fishing because he was futzing around so much with his individual zipper-top baggies and color-coded organizational system. Sometimes, when I'm using recipes from Carole Walter's *Great Cakes*, I think her subtitle should be *The Anal-Retentive Baker*. However, she didn't win a James Beard award for nothing. I've learned a lot from her directions, such as how to cream butter and sugar properly. The directions have been streamlined, but you'll find they're still pretty meticulous.

Spanish Meringue Cake serves about 12 people.

Spanish Meringue Cake — CONTINUED

4. In your mixer, using your regular paddle or beaters, cream the butter on medium speed, then gradually add the brown sugar, about 1 tablespoon at a time, mixing well. This should take 6 to 8 minutes. Don't forget to stop and scrape down the sides of the bowl.
5. In a separate bowl whisk together the flour, baking powder, and spices. Set aside.
6. Return to your fully creamed mixture and add the whole egg. Beat for 1 minute at medium speed. Add the egg yolks, one at a time, at 30-second intervals. Scrape the sides of the bowl occasionally. Beat for 1 minute before beating in the vanilla extract.
7. Reduce the mixer speed to low, and add a third of the flour mixture and half of the buttermilk and baking soda combo alternately, mixing until just incorporated. Repeat until all the flour mixture and buttermilk combo are just blended into the batter. Scrape down the sides of the bowl and mix for 10 seconds more.
8. Spoon the batter into the prepared pan, smoothing the surface with the back of a tablespoon. Sprinkle the chopped walnuts over the top and set aside.

TO MAKE THE MERINGUE

9. Replace the paddle with the whisk attachment.

   Clean and dry your mixing bowl, OR use an extra bowl that works with your mixer.
10. Beat the egg whites on medium speed until frothy.

NEW TECHNIQUE

BEATING EGG WHITES (AND SOME EGG WHITE TERMINOLOGY)

Frothy means like the head on a nice, tall glass of Guinness beer. This is denser than the "frothy" you get when you blow air through a straw in a glass of milk. The mixture will have bubbles and will be cloudy instead of clear. This is when salt or cream of tartar is added.

The next stage of beaten egg whites, *soft peak*, is so named because a peak forms when you lift the whisk out of the whites, then gracefully sinks back into the rest of whites. Soft peak stage is denser than "frothy" and it's the stage when sugar is usually added.

At the *firm peak* stage, that same "lift the whisk" maneuver leaves behind firm peaks that are well defined and don't sink back down. All of the egg whites are shiny and moist looking.

Stiff peak stage is a step beyond firm peak: the egg whites are very stiff and the meringue has gone beyond shiny to glossy. This stage happens when sugar has been added to the firm peak stage.

Overbeating past this stage will take you to the "flaccid peak" stage, which means it's time to dry your eyes, mend your heart, get new eggs, and start over.

That's your little primer on egg whites.

11. Add the cream of tartar and increase the mixer speed to medium-high. Beat to firm peaks.
12. Reduce the mixer to medium speed and add the brown sugar, 2 tablespoons at a time, beating until just blended. Add the spices and mix briefly. You should now have stiff peaks; be careful not to beat the meringue too much.
13. Using a spatula, gently mound the meringue on top of the batter in the cake pan. Use the back of a tablespoon to spread out the meringue evenly.
14. Center the pan on the rack (which, you remember, is in the lower third of the oven) and bake for 40 to 45 minutes, or until the cake begins to pull away from the sides of the pan and tests done. You may get a little meringue "cling" on your cake tester—ignore it. You're looking for the telltale *wet batter* cling, which by now, veteran of oh-so-many cakes, you know so well.
15. Allow the cake to cool in the pan, then remove the springform sides.

Now, Carole Walter adds this information: meringue-topped cakes will become soggy if air does not circulate around them. I made this cake the day before I took it into work. Instead of locking it tightly in my cake carry overnight, I propped the carry's lid up about $1/2$ inch from the bottom, and *ATC* did not suffer a soggy cake.

Honey Spice Cake with Rum Glaze

YOU'LL NEED

A 12-cup Bundt or 10-inch tube pan
A whisk attachment and extra bowl for mixer
A large spatula

FOR THE CAKE

½ cup sugar
1½ sticks (¾ cup) unsalted butter, at room temperature
⅔ cup clover honey
3 large egg yolks (see Tip)
2⅓ cups cake flour
1½ teaspoons baking powder
½ teaspoon baking soda
1 teaspoon ground ginger
1 teaspoon ground cinnamon
½ teaspoon ground cloves
½ teaspoon salt
1 cup plain yogurt
4 large egg whites (see Tip)

FOR THE GLAZE

1¼ cups confectioners' sugar
1½ tablespoons rum (light or dark)

Tip: Oh yes, you read this right: You're going to need 4 large eggs and you're going to have to separate them, but you're only going to use the yolks from 3 of them.

TO MAKE THE CAKE

1. Center a rack and preheat the oven to 350 degrees F. Prepare the Bundt or tube pan.
2. Set aside ¼ cup of the sugar.
3. Cream the butter with the mixer on medium speed until smooth. Gradually add the honey and the remaining ¼ cup of sugar and beat on high speed until smooth.
4. Reduce the speed to low and add the egg yolks, one at a time, beating after each addition.
5. In a separate bowl, dry whisk the cake flour, baking powder, baking soda, ginger, cinnamon, cloves, and salt together.
6. With the mixer on low speed, gradually add half of the flour mixture to the batter, followed by ½ cup of the yogurt, blending well after each addition. Repeat so that all of the flour mixture and yogurt are blended in. Increase the mixer speed to medium-high and beat until smooth.
7. Here's where having that whisk attachment and second bowl for your mixer comes in handy: Exchange the paddle or beaters for the whisk, and substitute a clean bowl for the one with the batter.
8. Beat the egg whites on medium-high speed to the soft peak stage.
9. Gradually add the reserved ¼ cup of sugar, then beat on high speed until stiff peaks form.
10. Gently fold the egg whites into the batter. This is the exact same folding technique you learned on page 62. The key here is to continue rotating the bowl until all the egg whites are incorporated. Don't be overly aggressive: You do not want to deflate the egg whites, but you do want to incorporate them into the batter evenly. It may take up to 15 full rotations of the bowl before this is done.
11. Pour the batter into the cake pan. Bake for 45 to 55 minutes, until the cake tests done.

12. Let the cake cool for 10 minutes in the pan; then unmold onto a cake rack. Allow to cool completely before finishing with the glaze.

TO MAKE THE GLAZE

13. In a small bowl, mix the confectioners' sugar and rum together to make a stiff glaze. If you'd like it looser, water it down with a teaspoon or so of milk.

TO FINISH THE CAKE

14. Put a plate under the cake and drizzle the glaze over the cake. Allow it to harden before serving.

This is my personal observation gleaned from trolling for recipes: Emeril Lagasse does not bake for more than six people at a time. This recipe came from the 2004 "Holiday Christmas Party" episode of *Emeril Live* on the Food Network. Apparently Emeril has only five cake-eating friends, because originally this was a tiny cake. A good cake, but a small one. Some of my co-workers made jokes about Emeril's wee cake for the rest of the week. Now, anytime I come across one of his cake recipes, I double it.

At this point, you're in good shape to try folding egg whites into batter. This is a technique that's going to come up a lot in the fancy-pants cake section of this book.

Holiday Honey Cake ANOTHER ADVENTURE IN RE-CAKING

YOU'LL NEED

A 12-cup Bundt pan or 10-inch tube pan
A whisk attachment and extra bowl for mixer
A large spatula

¾ cup sliced almonds
¾ cup honey
2 tablespoons Grand Marnier (see Wallet Warning)
1 tablespoon dark molasses
⅔ cup hot strong coffee
1 stick (½ cup) unsalted butter, at room temperature
½ cup brown sugar (light or dark)
2 large egg yolks
1 tablespoon vegetable oil
1 teaspoon grated orange zest
2¾ cups cake flour
1¼ teaspoons baking powder
½ teaspoon baking soda
¼ teaspoon salt
¾ teaspoon ground cinnamon
¼ teaspoon ground cloves
¼ teaspoon ground ginger
¼ teaspoon ground nutmeg
2 large egg whites
⅛ teaspoon cream of tartar

Wallet Warning: Liquor can be expensive, and if it's not something you normally keep stocked (I grew up in a nondrinking household, so a stocked bar is alien to me), here's a tip: I make several recipes with dark rum and brandy, so I buy medium-sized bottles and keep them on hand. The other liquors that find their way into my cakes—whiskey, bourbon, Grand Marnier, Bacardi rum, Kahlúa—I buy in those little, minibar-size plastic bottles. Takes up less space and less cash.

1. Center a rack and preheat the oven to 350 degrees F. Prepare the pan.
2. While the oven is preheating, spread out the almonds in a shallow baking pan and toast for 3 minutes. Remove from the oven, toss the almonds in the pan, then return to the oven for 3 more minutes. Set aside.
3. In a small bowl, stir together the honey, Grand Marnier, and molasses. Stir in the hot coffee, mix well, and set aside.
4. Cream the butter on medium speed, then gradually add the sugar, beating well after each addition. Add the egg yolk, one at a time, beating well after each addition.
5. Add the vegetable oil and orange zest and beat until smooth.
6. In a large mixing bowl, dry whisk the flour, baking powder, baking soda, salt, and spices together. Set aside.

7. Add a third of the flour mixture to the batter, half of the honey mixture, and beat until smooth. Repeat, and add the remainder of the flour mixture. Beat until smooth.
8. Set aside the bowl with the batter, and replace the paddle with the whisk attachment.
9. In a clean mixing bowl, beat the egg whites until frothy.
10. Add the cream of tartar to the egg whites and continue beating to the soft peak stage.
11. Using a spatula, fold half the egg whites into the batter, taking about 10 full turns, until incorporated.
12. Crush the toasted almonds into small pieces and sprinkle over the batter.
13. Fold in the remaining egg whites, taking about 15 full turns to incorporate.
14. Pour the batter into the pan and bake for 50 to 55 minutes, or until the cake tests done.
15. Cool the cake in the pan for 10 to 15 minutes. Unmold the cake onto a cake rack and cool completely.
16. Cover the cake: Lightly wrap with foil or seal in a plastic cake container and let the cake mature for 24 hours before serving.

Note: "Maturing" means that a cake is allowed to set, giving it time for all the spices and booze to really permeate the crumb.

So, it was Rosh Hashanah and I found a recipe for the occasion. It was advertised as a "moist, aromatic cake." I followed the original recipe to the letter, but the cake turned out utterly bland. My co-workers had very long faces, verily disappointed they were. All except Ari Shapiro, who told me it tasted like every Rosh Hashanah cake he'd ever had: more like overly dry Rosh Hashanah *bread*, he said, but as far as bread went, it wasn't that bad.

While *All Breads Considered* might very well be in my future, I opted to re-cake, adding two ingredients that I knew would lead to a moist cake: brown sugar and butter. The re-cake was a big hit.

The lesson here: never give up, never surrender. Especially when spice and vice and a holiday are involved.

This is a cake that needs to "mature" before serving. So make it a day ahead.

This cake has a delicate crumb, so expect to serve between 16 and 24 when you make it.

Araby Spice Cake

YOU'LL NEED

A 10-inch tube pan

FOR THE CAKE

1½ sticks (¾ cup) unsalted butter, at room temperature
1½ cups sugar
3 large eggs
2 cups cake flour
¼ teaspoon baking powder
½ teaspoon baking soda
¾ teaspoon salt
¾ teaspoon ground nutmeg
1 teaspoon ground cinnamon
2 tablespoons unsweetened cocoa
¾ cup buttermilk
1 teaspoon vanilla extract
1 teaspoon lemon juice

FOR THE FROSTING

6 tablespoons unsalted butter
1 large egg yolk
3 cups confectioners' sugar
1½ teaspoons unsweetened cocoa
1 teaspoon ground cinnamon
1½ teaspoons hot coffee (see Tip)

Tip: Remember what I said back in Coffee Spice Cake (page 98) about how older recipes are more apt to include coffee? And how my local Starbucks is next door to a nail salon? Well, this is our chance for a pedicure OR a grande mocha! Be wild. Go for Scarlett Red AND a grande mocha Frappuccino!

TO MAKE THE CAKE

1. Center a rack and preheat the oven to 350 degrees F. Prepare the cake pan.
2. Cream the butter at medium speed, then gradually add the sugar, mixing until smooth.
3. Add the eggs, one at a time, beating well after each addition.
4. In a separate bowl, dry whisk the flour, baking powder, baking soda, salt, spices, and cocoa together. Set aside.
5. In a small bowl, combine the buttermilk, vanilla extract, and lemon juice.
6. Add ½ cup of the flour mixture, beat, then add ¼ cup of the buttermilk mixture and beat again. Repeat until all of the flour mixture and buttermilk mixture are blended in. Beat on high speed for 1 additional minute.

7. Pour the batter into the baking pan and bake for about 45 minutes. Remove from the oven when the cake tests done.
8. Cool the cake in the pan for 10 minutes, then unmold onto a cake rack and cool completely.

TO MAKE THE FROSTING

9. With the mixer at medium speed, cream together the butter, egg yolk, confectioners' sugar, cocoa, cinnamon, and hot coffee. Blend until smooth.
10. Drizzle or spread the frosting on top of the cake.

I don't know WHY it's called "Araby" Spice Cake. I don't really know if "Araby" is a derogatory word in these times. I do know that back during the first few decades of the last century, Americans were FASCINATED by anything from the Middle East. Silent movies from the time featured Rudolph Valentino as The Sheik and Theda Bara, her eyes heavily kohled like those of an Egyptian queen. And speaking of Egyptian royalty, the news was full of stories about the discovery of King Tut's tomb. Everything "Arab" was hot, and "Araby" was the adjective of the day.

This is a recipe from Jane Marshall's home economics–teacher mother, Shirley Moser Marshall. Jane says they grew up on this cake, and that her mom probably got the recipe by way of Betty Crocker. It is tasty, especially to members of the Spice-and-Vice Alliance who crave chocolate every once in a while. So, call it what you like; hell, call it what it's really called and then call in the PC police while you're at it and when they arrive, shut them up with a slice of cake. We can be very PC at NPR, but if anyone was offended by this cake, I didn't hear about it.

You can expect to serve 16 to 24 uncomplaining people with this recipe.

Black Walnut Cake

SMELLS LIKE A PANCAKE, BUT TASTES LIKE A CAKE!

YOU'LL NEED

A 12-cup Bundt pan or 10-inch tube pan
A food processor, OR nut chopper, OR meat mallet

FOR THE CAKE

1 cup black walnuts
2 sticks (1 cup) unsalted butter, at room temperature
½ cup shortening
1½ cups brown sugar (light or dark)
1½ cups sugar
5 large eggs
3 cups all-purpose flour
1 teaspoon baking powder
½ teaspoon salt
1 cup milk
1 teaspoon vanilla extract

FOR THE GLAZE

1¼ cups confectioners' sugar
2 tablespoons unsalted butter
2 tablespoons milk
1 teaspoon maple extract

TO MAKE THE CAKE

1. Center a rack and preheat the oven to 350 degrees F. Prepare the pan.
2. Put the walnuts in a food processor. Pulse for about 45 seconds, or until the walnuts are finely chopped, but not pulverized.

   If you don't have a food processor, you can put the walnuts into a heavy zipper-top freezer bag, and close the bag all but 1 inch (so the air can escape). With a meat mallet or the back of a strong wooden spoon, release your pent-up anger and beat the devil out of the walnuts. Do not pulverize them, no matter how mad you feel. That's considered nut abuse, and we all know society frowns upon that.
3. With the mixer on medium speed, cream the butter and shortening together, then gradually add both sugars, about ½ cup at a time, beating well after each addition.

CONTINUED –

Black walnut is one of those "you either hate it or love it" flavors: it's stronger than regular walnut, with an earthy bite that's on the bitter side. It's such a divisive flavor that I send out an e-mail warning when I make one. I found out that our host Melissa Block HATES black walnuts. But she was in the minority; foodies Graham Smith and Ellen Silva declared it "superyummydelicious" and "wonderfully complex." That might be because I opted for two special techniques to dampen the shock of the black walnuts: chopping the hell out of them, then drizzling the cake with a sweet maple glaze.

Let me tell you something about black walnuts. They'll cost you about a dollar more per half cup than regular walnuts and here's why: a black walnut is a pretty hard nut to crack. The outer shell often grows around the meat inside the nut, making it darn near impossible to get out an entire kernel in one piece, the way you can English or Persian walnuts.

Black Walnut Cake was a favorite recipe of Grandma Gray's. She'd bake several every year to give away as Christmas gifts. She would also freeze them to use at a later date.

And I have to be honest, I never really liked Grandma's Black Walnut Cake. It just tasted like sour cream pound cake with walnuts in it. Too much sour, way too much bitter. So I nosed around on the Internet until I found this recipe from Allrecipes. It works well in a decorative Bundt, and it's really good warm, right out of the oven. Expect to serve between 16 and 24 people.

Black Walnut **Cake** — CONTINUED

4. Add the eggs, one at a time, beating well after each addition.
5. In a separate bowl, dry whisk the flour, baking powder, and salt together.
6. Add 1 cup of the flour mixture and ⅓ cup of the milk alternately, beating well after each addition, until all of the flour mixture and milk are blended in.
7. Add the vanilla extract and mix until blended. Set aside 1 tablespoon of the finely chopped black walnuts. Add the remaining black walnuts to the batter and mix on low speed until evenly distributed through batter.
8. Pour the batter into the prepared pan and bake for 1 hour, or until the cake tests done.
9. Allow to cool in pan for 10 minutes, then unmold onto a cake rack.

And, while the cake is cooling . . .

TO MAKE THE GLAZE

10. Put the confectioners' sugar in the bowl of the mixer. Then melt the butter in a saucepan over low heat. Beat in the melted butter, the milk, and maple extract, and beat until the mixture is smooth.

TO FINISH THE CAKE

11. Set a clean plate under the cake rack to catch drips. Spoon the glaze over the cake. Go all the way around once or twice, allowing the excess glaze to run down the sides and inside of the cake onto the plate below. With the reserved 1 tablespoon of finely chopped black walnuts, sprinkle the top of the cake evenly.

This cake is great served at room temperature or warm.

Banana Cake with Chocolate Frosting

SMELLS LIKE BANANA BREAD, BUT TASTES LIKE CAKE!

YOU'LL NEED

A 10-inch tube pan
A double boiler, real or improvised (see step 9)

FOR THE CAKE

2/3 cup shortening
1 2/3 cups sugar
2 1/2 cups cake flour
1 1/4 teaspoons baking powder
1 teaspoon baking soda
1 teaspoon salt
1 1/4 cups ripe bananas, mashed
1/3 cup buttermilk
2 large eggs
2/3 cup chopped walnuts (optional)

FOR THE FROSTING

Two 1-ounce squares unsweetened chocolate
1 1/2 teaspoons vanilla extract
6 tablespoons unsalted butter, at room temperature
4 3/4 cups confectioners' sugar
1/4 cup cream or sweetened condensed milk

TO MAKE THE CAKE

1. Center a rack and preheat the oven to 350 degrees F. Prepare the pan.
2. With the mixer on medium speed, cream the shortening, then gradually add the sugar, mixing well.
3. In a separate bowl, dry whisk the cake flour, baking powder, baking soda, and salt together. Add to the creamed mixture, beating until blended.
4. Add the mashed bananas and half the buttermilk and mix just until moistened, then increase the mixer speed to medium-high and beat for 2 minutes more.
5. Add the rest of the buttermilk and the eggs, and beat for 2 more minutes.
6. If you're going for the walnuts, add them to the batter and mix on low speed until just blended.
7. Pour the batter into the prepared pan. Bake for about 50 minutes, until the cake tests done.
8. Cool for 10 minutes , then unmold onto a cake rack and cool completely.

CONTINUED —

This was one of those special requests from a colleague who missed her mother. Carol Klinger's birthday was fast approaching one March when she asked if I could whip up a banana cake with chocolate frosting, just the way her late mother used to make. Turns out, Carol's mom loved baking and would do a custom cake for each of her children's birthdays. Carol loved the taste of bananas dipped in chocolate and rolled in nuts, like she'd had at Disneyland. So her mom would whip up her favorite flavors in a cake.

I'd never heard of banana cake before, let alone putting chocolate frosting on it, but I was interested in trying to re-create it for Carol. She works incredibly hard booking guests for the show, so I wanted to do her request justice. First, a little *CSI: Kitchen*. I got Carol to describe what she remembered of the flavor of the cake ("It was kind of like your banana bread, but cakier, with walnuts, and no booze") and the frosting ("She just did the top of the cake, not the sides. It was fudgy"). Then I baked two different cakes: a basic banana bread and this one, which comes from that '70s-era *Better Homes and Gardens New Cook Book*. Both had a thick, dark-chocolate icing just on the top of the cake. Carol had a slice of each, pronounced them "very good!" but said this was closest to the cake of her memory. Now, Banana Cake with Chocolate Frosting is on my list of must-do office cakes for the month of March, in honor of Carol and her mother.

This is a very easy recipe, which serves between 16 and 24 people. But be forewarned: it doesn't follow our standard mixing procedure!

Banana Cake with Chocolate Frosting — CONTINUED

TO MAKE THE FROSTING

9. Melt the chocolate in a double boiler or in a heat-proof bowl fitted into a saucepan with simmering water. Remove from the heat and stir in the vanilla extract. Allow to cool.
10. With the mixer on medium speed, cream the butter, then gradually add half of the confectioners' sugar, blending well. Beat in 2 tablespoons of cream. Beat in the remaining sugar and cream and set aside.
11. Add the melted chocolate to the creamed mixture and beat until smooth. Allow to cool slightly, then spread on the cooled cake.

Fresh Apple Cake

AH, YES, THIS IS ANOTHER FAMILY STORY

YOU'LL NEED

An 8-inch square or 9-inch round baking pan
A strong wooden spoon

2 cups sugar
3 large eggs
3 tablespoons vanilla extract
1 ½ cups vegetable oil
2 cups all-purpose flour
1 cup whole wheat flour
1 teaspoon baking soda
1 teaspoon ground cinnamon
1 teaspoon ground nutmeg
1 teaspoon salt
3 cups peeled and diced Granny Smith apples
1 cup raisins or dried cranberries or dried cherries
1 cup chopped walnuts

CONTINUED —

I mentioned that Grandma Gray would freeze her Black Walnut Cake (page 115). You might wonder why she'd do such a thing. Well, she'd been a farm woman all her adult life, and so whenever there was any extra food, it was dried, canned, smoked, or frozen and put up for the starving time surely to come. She was a bit manic about this. She was also very hospitable and would have died of embarrassment if someone showed up at her house and she had no cake to give them. I suppose to her, being caught without cake was like being caught tooling around the house in just your underpants. (My brother did catch her tooling around the house in just her shirt and underpants once. She was hot and wouldn't turn on the AC. But she did have cake.)

When my grandmother was in her heyday, people were always popping by the farm to visit, so she was always fully dressed (we like to think) and kept at least two cakes under wraps in the kitchen, with probably up to twenty in the cellar Deepfreeze, wrapped in wax paper and then tinfoil, with a little slip of paper tucked in, indicating what type of cake lay therein.

I exaggerate. It was likely fifteen cakes, not twenty.

Anyway, in addition to the Black Walnut Cake and her sour cream pound cake (page 17) and the occasional coconut cake that she liked to make to torment my brother (who hated coconut), she also made "fresh" apple cake with these little hard green apples from her apple trees. Actually, it would be more accurate to call it defrosted apple cake. I don't think I ever had one that was straight out of the oven. She was always worried about food going bad, so she would bake a fresh one and then, as soon as it cooled, she'd wrap it up and exchange it for an old one in the freezer. But she'd still ask you, "Would you like a slice of fresh apple cake?"

Why, yes I would. And in an hour and a half, I shall have one.

I adapted this recipe from one in *Sharing Our Best*, the community cookbook from the good folks at Providence Baptist Church in Gloucester, Virginia. It serves about 16.

Fresh Apple Cake — CONTINUED

1. Center a rack and preheat the oven to 350 degrees F. Prepare the cake pan.
2. In a mixer on medium speed, beat together the sugar, eggs, vanilla, and oil until well blended. The mixture will be . . . yes . . . oily.
3. In a separate bowl, dry whisk the flours, baking soda, cinnamon, nutmeg, and salt together.
4. Slow your mixer to low and add the flour mixture to the oily mixture in thirds, blending well after each addition.
5. Stop the mixer. The consistency of your batter may alarm you: it will be dense, slightly wetter than putty. Be not afraid. This cake will have heavy fruit in it (apples), so the batter needs to be very sturdy.
6. Add the apples and use a strong wooden spoon to fold them into the batter. Add the dried fruit and walnuts and fold them into the batter.
7. Getting this batter into the cake pan is closer to dumping than pouring and will require what I call the double-fisted, hearty wooden-spoon-and-spatula method, because it IS heavy and it IS sticky and your heart will be pumping! Let your wooden spoon do most of the job, then use your spatula to scrape excess batter from the bowl and the spoon.
8. Bake for 1 hour. When the cake tests done, let cool for 15 minutes and unmold onto a cake rack to finish cooling.
9. Now, this cake has a cookielike crust and is moderately sweet. If you need more sweet, you can dust with confectioners' sugar OR you can drizzle with honey. You'll find this baby is particularly good fresh and warm on cold fall mornings when you're trying to defrost your own fine self.

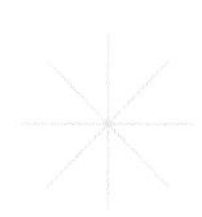

The fruit voted "MR. POPULARITY" BAKED APPLE

It's not an exaggeration; 99 percent of my coworkers agree that baked apples are da bomb. It's not just the taste, but the smell and, methinks, the idea that they're eating healthy because there's fruit in every bite. After all, apples contain vitamin C, fiber, and antioxidants; surely that must counterbalance all that sugar and oil in the cake!

Korva Coleman, keep telling yourself that.

Apples are deliciously utilitarian in and of themselves, but when baked, they become both homey and festive. Part of this has to do with the time of year when they're in high season: September through November. You've got Rosh Hashanah, during which apples with honey symbolize a sweet new year; followed by Halloween, with its candy apples; and then Thanksgiving, which to some is incomplete without apple pie. Good times and nice warm feelings, unless your family drives you crazy or you're not particularly into holidays.

Regardless, you probably do like apples, and you've got a wide variety to choose from. There are more than seven thousand different types of apples in the world, though chances are your local grocery store stocks only half a dozen types.

Rome Beauty is considered the queen of the bakers, because cooking really brings out that apply flavor. But if you like strongly tart and firm, go for Granny Smith. Prefer sweet and a little softer? Try Golden Delicious. Want a nice blend of sweet and tart and firm? Braeburns and Cortlands are good choices. How about sweet and soft? Go for Gala.

I did a taste test at *ATC* one Monday with four Fresh Apple Cakes (page 119), each with a different apple: Fuji, Gala, Granny Smith, and Braeburn. Granny Smith and Braeburn were the clear favorites, and someone suggested combining them in one cake next time.

You'll find that most apples do fine when baked, with one universal exception: Red Delicious. This really sweet variety is drop-dead, smack-that-wicked-Disney-step-mother gorgeous, but it gets rather mushy under heat, so avoid it for anything other than your lunch box, snacks, or salads.

Apples are available year-round because they're very easy to store. In fact, you can keep them for weeks in a plastic bag in the refrigerator. They might get mealy after a while, but they'll still be edible.

Paula Deen's Grandgirl's Fresh Apple Cake from Georgia

COCONUT HATERS BEWARE—YOU MIGHT ACTUALLY LIKE THIS CAKE

YOU'LL NEED

A 10-inch tube pan
A medium saucepan
The nonbusiness end of a wooden spoon

FOR THE CAKE

3 cups all-purpose flour
1 teaspoon baking soda
¼ teaspoon salt
1 tablespoon ground cinnamon
2 cups sugar
3 large eggs
1½ cups vegetable oil
¼ cup orange juice
1 tablespoon vanilla extract
3 cups peeled and chopped apples
1 cup unsweetened shredded coconut (I prefer to shred it further in the food processor)
1 cup chopped pecans

FOR THE SAUCE

1 stick (½ cup) unsalted butter
1 cup sugar
½ cup buttermilk
½ teaspoon baking soda

TO MAKE THE CAKE

1. Position a rack so the cake will sit in the middle of the oven, and preheat to 325 degrees F. Prepare the cake pan.
2. In a separate bowl, dry whisk the flour, baking soda, salt, and cinnamon together.
3. OH THIS PART IS SO MUCH FUN!

   In the bowl of a mixer, dump the sugar, eggs, oil, your dry ingredients mixture, orange juice, and the vanilla. Yes, dump them! All together! Then mix on medium speed until blended.
4. Fold in the apples, coconut, and pecans.
5. Pour the batter into the prepared tube pan and bake for 1 hour and 30 minutes, or until the cake tests done. Shortly before the cake is done, make the sauce.

TO MAKE THE SAUCE

6. Melt the butter in a medium saucepan over medium heat. Stir in the sugar, buttermilk, and baking soda.
7. Bring the mixture to a rolling boil, stirring constantly. Boil for 1 full minute, then remove from the heat.

TO FINISH THE CAKE

8. I LOVE THIS PART, TOO!!

   With the hot cake still in the pan, take the handle of the wooden spoon (the nonbusiness end) and poke about 15 to 20 holes through the top of the cake. Then pour the sauce over the hot cake.

9. Let the cake stand for 1 hour in the pan before unmolding it onto a cake rack.

It will be moist. It will be sticky. It will be oh, so very gooooooooooood.

And why? Because coconut is not the predominant flavor or texture. To paraphrase President Bill Clinton's unofficial campaign slogan from 1992, "It's the fresh apples, stupid."

I nabbed this recipe from *Paula's Home Cooking* on the Food Network. It comes from her "Southern Seafood Show."

I love this cake. It's one of the three cakes I knew how to do long before I embarked upon the Cake Project, and as I wrote in the introduction to this book, it's so easy a drunken monkey can't mess it up. It's a good cake for skeptics because you get to poke holes in it, too.

Do not bake this in a Bundt—you might as well take a meat mallet and smack yourself between the eyes with it. That's the kind of headache you'd be in for. Instead, use a straight-sided tube pan. And, since this cake is best served in thick slices, plan on treating 16 to 20 people.

Peach Cake with Cream Cheese Frosting

YET ANOTHER SCORE FOR THOSE SMALL-TOWN, COMMUNITY COOKBOOKS!

YOU'LL NEED

A 10-inch tube pan

FOR THE CAKE

3 large eggs, beaten
1¾ cups sugar
1 cup vegetable oil
2 cups all-purpose flour
1 teaspoon salt
1 teaspoon baking soda
1 teaspoon ground cinnamon
2 cups sliced peaches, preferably canned
½ cup chopped nuts (optional)

FOR THE FROSTING

3 ounces cream cheese, at room temperature
4 tablespoons unsalted butter, at room temperature
1 teaspoon vanilla extract
2 cups confectioners' sugar
½ teaspoon ground ginger

TO MAKE THE CAKE

1. Center a rack and preheat the oven to 375 degrees F. Prepare the cake pan.
2. In the bowl of a mixer, combine the eggs, sugar, and oil. Mix on medium speed until just blended.
3. In a separate bowl, dry whisk the flour, salt, baking soda, and cinnamon together. Add to the egg mixture and beat until just combined. The batter will be sticky.
4. With a spatula and/or wooden spoon, fold in the peaches and nuts.
5. Pour the batter into the prepared cake pan and bake for 50 minutes, or until the cake tests done.
6. Let the cake cool for 10 minutes in the pan, then unmold onto a cake rack. Allow to cool completely.

TO MAKE THE FROSTING

7. With the mixer on medium speed, beat the cream cheese, butter, and vanilla extract until smooth.
8. Gradually add the confectioners' sugar and ginger. Beat until smooth.
9. Apply the frosting to the cooled cake.

One of my uncles, in his predictably sexist way (yes, Uncle Johnny, I'm talking about you), once remarked that he wished women didn't work, because the food at church dinners wasn't very good anymore. "What's wrong with your hands?" I asked. "You're retired. You can read a cookbook, can't you?" He thought I was joking. Ha! I wasn't. And I'm starting to think a copy of my now favorite community cookbook, *Sharing Our Best*, from the Providence Baptist Church of Gloucester, Virginia, would be a mighty fine Christmas gift for him. This book is fabulous!

And this peach cake recipe is the big-time winner of all the cake recipes, as far as I'm concerned. I don't know who Tina Mongold Bryner is, but she's got my eternal blessing for including this recipe in the collection. I've done it with both canned and fresh peaches, and I have to say I preferred the results with the canned peaches. The key is to rinse the syrup off before you add the peaches to the mixing bowl.

Just like Paula Deen's Grandgirl's Fresh Apple Cake (page 122), you don't have to be anal retentive with the mixing. Frankly, my dear, the only thing that takes time is rinsing and slicing the peaches. This cake should be served in thick slices, so plan on feeding 16 to 20.

Faux Fruitcake

A FRUITCAKE FOR THOSE WHO DESPISE FRUITCAKE

YOU'LL NEED

2 loaf pans or a 10-inch tube pan
A strong wooden spoon

FOR THE CAKE

1 pound orange slices gummy candy, cut up in smaller pieces
One 8-ounce package chopped dates
2 cups walnuts, finely chopped
1½ cups unsweetened shredded coconut
½ cup all-purpose flour
2 sticks (1 cup) unsalted butter, at room temperature
2 cups sugar
4 large eggs
1 teaspoon baking soda
¾ cup buttermilk
½ teaspoon salt
3½ cups all-purpose flour

FOR THE GLAZE

1 cup orange juice
2 cups confectioners' sugar

TO MAKE THE CAKE

1. Center a rack and preheat the oven to 300 degrees F. Prepare the cake pans.
2. Combine the orange candy, dates, walnuts, coconut, and flour in a bowl and set aside.
3. Cream the butter with a mixer on medium speed. Gradually add the sugar, beating well. Add the eggs, one at a time, beating well after each addition.
4. In a separate small bowl, mix the baking soda with the buttermilk.
5. In a medium bowl, dry whisk the salt and flour together.
6. Add half the flour mixture and half the buttermilk mixture alternately, beating well after each addition, and repeat.
7. Using a strong wooden spoon, fold in the fruit and nut mixture.
8. Pour the batter into the prepared pans and bake for 1 hour and 45 minutes if you're using a tube pan, and 1 hour and 20 minutes for the loaf pans.

TO MAKE THE GLAZE

9. About 10 minutes before the cake is ready to come out of the oven, combine the orange juice and confectioners' sugar in the bowl of a mixer, beating until smooth.

TO FINISH THE CAKE

10. Once the cake is out of the oven and still hot, use a skewer to poke small holes through the top of the cake. Pour the glaze over the cake. Allow it to fully absorb the glaze, then carefully unmold onto a cake rack to cool. The cake will be sticky.

Carl Kasell isn't one of them. Our veteran newscaster loves fruitcake. But he's in the minority among those of us who typically work the holidays at NPR.

We get double-time-and-a-half on Christmas and New Year's, and usually they're each a snoozer of a news day. But like firemen and police, we have to staff the holidays anyway, just in case. Just in case Boris Yeltsin resigns (which he did New Year's Eve 1999) or James Brown dies (which he did Christmas 2006). We sit around our computers, all casual in jeans and sweaters or sweatshirts, and even though we're at work, we do try to enjoy the day. And that means going on a movable feast. Actually, it's more like a movable graze: we spend the entire day noshing from unit to unit. It starts with *Morning Edition*, where someone like editor Doreen MaCallister will have a Crock-Pot set up with creamed corn beef or a spread of crackers, cheese, and summer sausage. Then between Newscast and *All Things Considered*, someone has cider or eggnog, someone else has more smoked sausage and an array of cheeses and crackers, and there are plenty of cakes and cookies to share with the IT guys and the engineers, not to mention Hershey's Kisses and candy canes. *ATC* usually gets Chinese food for lunch, and by the time the work day is over, we're all just as overstuffed and lethargic as if we'd spent the day at home with our blood relations.

I always bake cookies for work during the holidays—sugar cookies, Cowboy Cookies (page 137), gingersnaps, Oatmeal Cherry Cookies (page 139)—but sometimes I bake Faux Fruitcake, if only to get the NPR holiday staffers to renounce their fruitcake-hating ways. Even though I've got a sterling reputation as far as baking goes, I was surprised how many people I had to browbeat into trying this cake. They kept thinking it was like the typical fruitcake of yore: hard as a brickbat, sticky as the glue NASA uses on the tiles of the space shuttle, and preserved better than Twinkies. But the people who tried it were surprised at how much they liked it.

I had the same reaction when my Aunt Janet first gave me this recipe. My only quibble is with the quality of the candy orange slices I used: I think they were kind of old, because they were rather hard. This made cutting the cake an exercise in how-to-properly-use-a-fulcrum. So, tip number 1 is to feel your candy orange slices through the bag before you buy them and make sure they're not rock hard. Tip number 2: Use a good pair of kitchen shears to cut the orange candy, dusting the blades with flour about every third snip. Tip number 3: Use a sharp knife to slice your finished cake, and please cut THIN slices: you don't want to effect a sugar coma on your guests or coworkers.

This cake serves as many as you can sweet-talk into eating it.

Martha Washington's Great Cake

THE CAKE THAT LAUNCHED THE CAKE PROJECT AND THIS HERE BOOK!

YOU'LL NEED

A 10-inch tube pan
Whisk attachment for mixer
A hand-held mixer (or an extra bowl for stand mixer)

FOR THE CAKE

10 large eggs
4 sticks (2 cups, aka 1 pound) unsalted butter, at room temperature
2 cups plus 2 tablespoons sugar
5 cups all-purpose flour
2½ teaspoons ground mace
2½ teaspoons ground nutmeg
¼ cup wine (recipe doesn't specify white or red; I use white)
¼ cup French brandy
1¼ pounds assorted fruits and nuts, chopped or sliced (about 18 ounces fruit and 2 ounces nuts, see Tip)

FOR THE FROSTING

3 large egg whites
1½ cups confectioners' sugar
1 teaspoon grated lemon zest
2 tablespoons orange extract

CONTINUED –

I live about five miles from Mount Vernon, and about every other fall, my husband, Jimmy, and I do the candlelight tour. The docents, dressed in period costumes, take you through what would have been a typical Christmas holiday with George and Martha. The two were besieged by guests every year, and you get the impression that George would have preferred his peace and quiet after he'd retired from the presidency. But social rules were social rules, so when people came calling, he was obliged to entertain.

The first room you enter is the dining room, and a woman dressed as Martha welcomes you from a comfy chair and explains how tired she is from everyone she's seen during the twelve-day holiday. She's quite jolly, slightly gossipy, and very engaging. She'll usually pick out a young girl from the group and ask her name. Whatever the child says (Emily, Lashelle, Madison), she'll exclaim, "Oh! What a FINE Virginia name!" And then she'll talk about this big white cake sitting on the dining room table.

It's iced in white, and it's made of seasonal fruits and brandy. But it's not a Christmas cake. It's an anniversary cake. The Washingtons were married on January 6, 1759, the traditional Twelfth Day of Christmas. With all the goings-on at Mount Vernon, both George and Martha looked forward to sharing a slice of the great cake to celebrate their mutual devotion and (one hopes) an emptying house.

This comes from a modern adaptation of Martha's original recipe, which was preserved for posterity by her granddaughter. The Mount Vernon Ladies' Association happily hands it out to visitors every holiday season.

This cake is a bit onerous: You've got to wrestle with egg whites, plus there's a lot of peeling and chopping. Because the cake goes back INTO the oven once you've iced it, I recommend that you be extra careful not to overbake it the first time. But it is a fun cake to do, and I especially like baking it during that lull between Christmas and New Year's, when everybody is mellow and relaxed. Plus, people seem to love the idea of eating what George Washington might have eaten, though they do seem to enjoy eating it with a full set of teeth.

This is a really dense cake, and it shouldn't be sliced too thickly. With a sharp knife, you can expect to feed between 20 and 28.

CONTINUED –

Martha Washington's Great Cake — CONTINUED

Tip: OK, here's a baking headache: a cup of one fruit or nut doesn't necessarily equal, in weight, a cup of another fruit or nut. You can Google, but here's a very, very brief guide:

1 pound (16 ounces) hazelnuts = 3 cups
1 pound pecans, almonds, or walnuts = 3⅛ cups
1 pound apples, chopped = 3 cups
1 pound apricots, sliced = 2⅛ cups
1 pound apricots, dried = 3¼ cups
1 pound pears, sliced = 2 cups
1 pound dates, dried and chopped = 4 cups
1 pound figs, dried and chopped = 2⅔ cups
1 pound raisins, dried cherries, or dried cranberries = 3 cups

I leave you to do the math.

Here's another cheat sheet, courtesy of our dear friends at Mount Vernon, of what would have been available to Mrs. Martha during the holiday season:

5 ounces pear, peeled, cored, and diced
3½ ounces raisins
9½ ounces apples, peeled, cored, and diced
2 ounces sliced almonds

You'll have to do more math to tally 1¼ pounds (20 ounces) of your assorted fruits. Sorry. I never told you math was not involved in baking.

TO MAKE THE CAKE

1. Position a rack so the cake will sit in the middle of the oven, and pre-heat the oven to 350 degrees F. Prepare the pan.
2. Separate the egg whites from the yolks, collecting the egg whites in the bowl of a mixer, and set the yolks aside.
3. Using the whisk attachment on the mixer, whisk the egg whites to the soft peak stage.
4. In a separate mixing bowl, cream the butter with a handheld mixer. Slowly fold in a third of the beaten egg whites until incorporated. Repeat two times, until all the egg whites are incorporated.
5. Slowly fold in the sugar, about 1 cup at a time, until incorporated.

6. Beat the egg yolks lightly (you may use a hand whisk) and fold them in. Fold in the flour until fully incorporated.
7. Fold in the mace, nutmeg, wine, and brandy.
8. Fold in the fruits and nuts.
9. Pour the batter into the pan and bake for about 1 hour and 15 minutes, until the cake tests done.
10. Cool the cake in the pan for 10 minutes, then unmold onto a cake rack.

TO MAKE THE FROSTING

11. When the cake is almost cool, preheat the oven to 200 degrees F and make the frosting.
12. Using a hand mixer (or your arms, if you've had your vitamins), beat together the egg whites and 2 tablespoons of the confectioners' sugar. Continue adding the sugar, 2 tablespoons at a time, beating after each addition, until you have incorporated all of the sugar.
13. Add the grated lemon zest and orange extract flavoring. Beat until the frosting is stiff enough to stay parted when cut through with a knife.

TO FINISH THE CAKE

14. Smooth the meringue onto the cake. Let it dry and harden in the oven for 1 hour. The frosting will be brittle when cut with a knife.

Chapter Three

BREAK FROM CAKE

Oh, you'd better believe it happens . . .

THE MISTRESS OF CAKE SOMETIMES GETS SICK OF CAKE

ACTUALLY, IT'S A JONESING FOR SOMETHING ELSE, LIKE WHEN YOU'VE BEEN DATING THE SAME GUY FOR TWO YEARS AND YOU'RE NOT SURE IF YOU WANT TO MOVE IN WITH HIM OR MARRY HIM, AND THEN GEORGE CLOONEY OR TAYE DIGGS WALKS BY.

This happens every December for me. Not George and Taye (I wish), but the itch for something else. I cheat on my weekly cakes and do nothing but cookies. Sure, I bring in the Faux Fruitcake on Christmas Day, but leading up to that are Mondays of sugar cookies, gingersnaps, pecan sandies, Salty Oatmeal Cookies (page 140), Cowboy Cookies (page 137), Peanut Butter Fingers (page 138) and rugelach.

And about once every couple of months I go through two or three weeks of baking scones, biscotti, or bar cookies. And every now and then the *ATC* staff will look at me sweetly, and beg for Fried Pies (page 144).

With these moments in mind, I impart to you a few of my favorite noncake baked items. Other favorites you can find by investing in two books: *Dorie Greenspan's Baking: From My Home to Yours* (Dorie's scones makes you want to don a tartan and adopt a deep, rolling Edinburgh brogue) and the latest edition of *The Better Homes and Gardens New Cook Book* (still including cookie recipes from forty years ago, bless their red-and-white checkered hearts!).

Cowboy Cookies

YOU'LL NEED
Parchment paper
2 baking sheets
A metal spatula

1 cup sugar
1 cup brown sugar (light or dark)
1 cup shortening
2 large eggs, beaten
1 teaspoon vanilla extract
2 cups all-purpose flour
1 teaspoon baking soda
½ teaspoon salt
2 cups old-fashioned rolled oats (not quick-cooking)
1½ cups mixed morsels and/or nuts of your choice (see Tip)

Tip: Try ¾ cup bittersweet chocolate morsels and ¾ cup hazelnuts. Or ½ cup walnuts, ½ cup dried cherries, and ½ cup butterscotch chips. Go for 1 cup raisins and ½ cup white chocolate. These are just suggestions. Do what you like. It's your cookie!

1. Center a rack and preheat the oven to 350 degrees F. Trim the parchment paper to fit the baking sheets; you will thank me later. Using parchment paper instead of greasing the baking sheets makes for a SUPER easy cleanup.
2. Combine the sugars and shortening in the bowl of a mixer, and beat on medium speed until blended. Add the eggs and beat until blended. Add the vanilla extract and beat briefly.
3. In a separate bowl, dry whisk the flour, baking soda, and salt together. Add to the creamed mixture, beating on low to medium speed to blend.
4. Add the oats, beating until they are mixed into the dough.
5. Add no more than a total of 1½ cups of morsels, nuts, and dried fruit.
6. Drop the cookies by the teaspoon onto the baking sheets: you'll get about 9 per sheet.
7. Bake one sheet of cookies for 10 to 12 minutes, until the cookies are golden brown. Remove from the oven, and put in the sheet of unbaked cookies.
8. Use a spatula to transfer the baked cookies to a cooling rack. Let the baking sheet cool for 5 minutes, then measure out the next batch of cookies. When the parchment paper comes out browning around the edges, replace with a new sheet of paper.

These cookies became a family Christmas tradition in 1988. Mom found the recipe in the newspaper. With all the baking we did (and still do) around the holidays, we always seemed to have extra chips, nuts, and raisins left over. It was kind of a pain, having to tie up all these little bags, with no immediate option for using them up.

Hah! Not anymore. The beauty of these cookies is that the dough is easily adaptable to all those bits and pieces. You can create whatever flavor combination you desire: Want chocolate chips and nuts? Go for it. Or how about dried cherries instead of nuts? Have at it. Want white chocolate chips and macadamia nuts? Hey, it's your dime. Just make sure to share.

The main thing to remember is not to overdo the additions, or the batter will get quite crumbly. Depending on how big you make them, this recipe should produce about 2 dozen cookies.

Peanut Butter Fingers

This was my comfort sweet in college, and practically the only thing I baked on my own until I got into graduate school. The recipe comes from my mom's old 1953 edition of the *Better Homes and Gardens New Cook Book*. My 1971 edition and the 2007 edition don't include it, and the piece of scratch paper with the recipe on it, which I've been carrying around for twenty years, has browned with all the butter stains of my Peanut Butter Fingers past. At least I can honestly say my handwriting's gotten a lot better since freshman year.

This will serve about 16, or 1 if you're feeling selfish. I frequently am.

YOU'LL NEED

A 9-inch square baking pan

½ cup unsalted butter, at room temperature
½ cup sugar
½ cup brown sugar
1 large egg
⅓ cup peanut butter (crunchy!)
½ teaspoon vanilla extract
1 cup all-purpose flour
½ teaspoon baking soda
¼ teaspoon salt
1 cup old-fashioned rolled oats (not quick-cooking)

1. Center a rack and preheat the oven to 350 degrees F. Prepare the pan with baking spray.
2. With the mixer on medium speed, cream together the butter and sugars. Add the egg and beat well. Add the peanut butter and then the vanilla extract and beat well.
3. In a separate bowl, dry whisk the flour, baking soda, and salt together. Shift the mixer to low speed and add the dry ingredients to the creamed mixture, beating well.
4. Add the oats and mix well.
5. Spoon the batter into the prepared pan and smooth it out with a spatula. Bake for 20 to 25 minutes. Test like you would a cake, inserting a thin knife or toothpick in the center.
6. Remove from the oven and cool in the pan for 10 minutes before attempting to unmold onto a wire rack, or before cutting into bars in the pan. These are good warm, by the way.

Oatmeal Cherry Cookies

YOU'LL NEED

Parchment paper
2 baking sheets
A metal spatula

1¾ cups all-purpose flour
1 teaspoon baking soda
½ teaspoon ground cinnamon
Pinch of salt
2 sticks (1 cup) unsalted butter, at room temperature
1⅓ cups light brown sugar
⅓ cup sugar
2 large eggs
¼ cup milk
1 teaspoon vanilla extract
2½ cups old-fashioned rolled oats (not quick-cooking)
½ cup dried cherries
½ cup butterscotch morsels

1. Center a rack and preheat the oven to 350 degrees F. Trim the parchment paper to fit the baking sheets.
2. Dry whisk the flour, baking soda, cinnamon, and salt together. Set aside.
3. With the mixer on medium speed, cream together the butter and sugars until light and fluffy. Add the eggs, one at a time, and then the milk and vanilla extract, beating well.
4. On low speed, gradually add the flour mixture, beating well after each addition.
5. Slow the mixer down to low speed, add the oats, and beat until just mixed. Add the cherries and butterscotch morsels, mixing until just incorporated.
6. Using a teaspoon, drop the cookie dough onto the prepared baking sheets so they're evenly spaced, about 9 cookies per sheet.
7. Bake the first sheet of cookies for about 10 minutes, until golden brown.
8. Transfer the cookies to a rack to cool and put the next batch in the oven.

A winner from Shelia Lukins's *U.S.A. Cookbook* and a favorite of my father, my father-in-law, and my cake-hating husband, all of whom are named James, oddly enough. My brother, also a James, prefers heavy pound cake to all else, so no cookies for him. My nephew is a James, too, but he hasn't developed baked-goods preferences yet. I'll keep you posted. And, by the way, my son is named Thomas, not James.

This is an aromatic cookie, what with the brown sugar and spices. The only change I made to Shelia's recipe was the addition of butterscotch morsels, which give cookie-eaters an occasional extra-sweet surprise.

Salty Oatmeal Cookies

YOU'LL NEED

A medium saucepan
Parchment paper
2 baking sheets
A metal spatula

3 tablespoons unsalted butter
3 cups old-fashioned rolled oats (not quick-cooking)
¾ cup butter-flavored Crisco shortening
1 cup light brown sugar
½ cup sugar
1 teaspoon baking powder
¼ teaspoon baking soda
¼ teaspoon salt
½ teaspoon ground cinnamon
2 large eggs
1 teaspoon vanilla extract
½ teaspoon coconut extract
1¾ cups rice flour
Kosher salt, for sprinkling

1. In a medium saucepan, melt the butter. Remove from the heat and stir in the oats. Set aside.
2. With the mixer, beat the shortening on medium-high speed until light and fluffy. Scrape down the sides of the bowl and add the sugars gradually, beating until mixed.
3. In a separate bowl, dry whisk the baking powder, baking soda, salt, and cinnamon together. Add to the creamed mixture and beat until incorporated.
4. Add the eggs, vanilla extract, and coconut extract, beating until blended.
5. Reduce the mixer speed to low and add the oatmeal and the rice flour, scraping down the sides of the bowl and beating until just incorporated. Cover the bowl with plastic wrap and refrigerate the dough for at least 1 hour.
6. About 15 minutes before you're ready to bake, center a rack and preheat the oven to 375 degrees F. Cut out parchment paper to fit the cookie sheets.
7. Form the dough into balls the size of a golf ball and place on the baking sheets about 2 inches apart. Flatten the balls slightly and sprinkle generously with kosher salt.
8. Bake one sheet of cookies at a time for 15 minutes, or until the cookies are puffed and starting to turn golden brown.
9. With a spatula, transfer the cookies to a cooling rack.

OK, so there's this snooty little high-priced Asian-esque eatery in Washington, DC, where they serve a lot of tea. Some folks love it. I hate it. I always leave feeling hungry and not good enough because I'm too plebeian to be satisfied with a finger-sized portion of meat over three pieces of shredded lettuce and some bean sprouts. I also leave feeling amazingly cheap because I think paying more than $1.75 for a cup of tea is ridiculous. But that's just me. I have issues. You're reading this book and you know that. We're friends, you and I.

Well, this place also has these incredible Salty Oatmeal Cookies. I usually can't stand salty snacks, but BOY are these things dee-licious! They're big, they're doughy, they're sweet, they're cinnamony, they're salty. Thing is, the people who make these cookies for the restaurant won't give out the recipe.

In comes Leigh Lambert, staff writer for the *Washington Post*. She writes an article chronicling her attempt to crack the Salty Oatmeal Cookie Code. Trouble is, you read the article thinking you are going to end up with a recipe that was close to what you could buy (at the cost of a donor kidney on the black market) at the snooty little high-priced Asian-esque eatery. WRONG! After much searching Leigh settles on the cookie recipe that works for her. I tried it and it tastes like every oatmeal cookie I've ever had, except it's dusted with salt.

I was deeply miffed, perturbed, provoked, VEXED with Leigh for wasting my time. I could have just as easily baked Shelia Lukins's recipe for Oatmeat Cherry Cookies (page 139), minus the dried cherries and butterscotch morsels, and thrown kosher salt on them; I would have had the same cookie. When I get mad, I curse like a sailor. And then I set my jaw and get to work. The *Washington Post* food section be damned! I was now determined to crack the Salty Oatmeal Cookie code on my own.

It took me four tries and our staff weighed in at every turn. The first problem I saw with Leigh's recipe is that it called for butter, not shortening. The real SOCs had a slightly crumbly, light texture similar to Cowboy Cookies (page 137), which have shortening. Ellen Silva, our commentaries editor, surmised this might be a key ingredient in the real SOCs and indeed, if the original bakers used shortening, it made sense that they might not want to give out that information since the snooty little high-priced Asian-esque eatery has a healthy reputation. I tried the shortening and added an extra cup of oats. The texture improved, but the taste did not. I switched to a new product put out by Crisco, butter-flavored shortening. The taste got closer.

Senior producer Graham Smith was now eating cookies by the fistful and telling me I could stop; these were perfect! Brendan Banaszak, another producer, disagreed, noting that they were GOOD, but the texture was still slightly off.

Rereading Leigh's article, I noticed that she'd replaced the rice flour in the real SOCs (listed on the back of the cookie wrapper) with regular flour, so I reverted back to rice flour. Sara Sarasohn, our West Coast arts editor, suggested adding coconut extract. Closer, closer, but still not there. Part of the cookie's taste, Leigh believed, had to do with refrigerating the dough for at least an hour before baking, allowing the oats to absorb moisture and flavor from the eggs and butter. I tried that. I decided to toss the oats in 2 tablespoons of melted butter BEFORE introducing them into the dough. WUNDERBAR!

At this point, Graham and Brendan and Ellen all told me to STOP; they loved the cookies just the way they were and even if I couldn't fully crack the real SOC code, they liked what I had better than the cookies from the snooty little high-priced Asian-esque eatery. They grabbed several each and took them back to their desks to store them for deadline sugar 'n' salt emergencies and then demanded the recipe, which I happily gave up for free as I have no need for donor kidneys. Then the rest of the staff, who had kept silent in hopes that I wouldn't crack the real SOC code so that I'd bake all week, asked if I was still going to bring in more cookies the next day.

This recipe makes 2 dozen cookies, but if you like 'em big, you'll obviously get fewer cookies. Be forewarned—the bigger you make them, the more they spread on the sheet, so space accordingly!

Chewy Butterscotch Bars

YOU'LL NEED

A 9 x 13-inch baking pan or two 8-inch round cake pans
A baking sheet
A double boiler, real or improvised (see step 4)

2 cups coarsely chopped or broken pecans
1½ cups all-purpose flour
1 teaspoon baking powder
¼ teaspoon salt
4 large eggs
1 teaspoon instant espresso powder (see Tip)
2 cups dark brown sugar
2 tablespoons unsalted butter, cut into small pieces
2 teaspoons vanilla extract
½ cup butterscotch morsels

Tip: I use instant coffee. Works just as well.

1. Center a rack and preheat the oven to 350 degrees F. Prepare the pan.
2. Spread out the pecans in a single layer on a baking sheet and toast in the oven for about 3 minutes. Toss and stir, then toast for 3 more minutes. Set aside on a plate to cool to room temperature.
3. In a large bowl, dry whisk the flour, baking powder, and salt together; set aside.
4. Bring about 1 inch of water to a boil in the bottom of your double boiler, OR in a saucepan into which you can insert a heat-proof bowl so that it will not touch the water. Reduce the water to a simmer.
5. Away from the heat, in the top of the double boiler (or in the bowl), whisk the eggs just enough to combine the yolks and whites.
6. Whisk in the espresso powder (or instant coffee). Whisking constantly, add the sugar and continue whisking until completely smooth. Add the butter.
7. Place the top of the double boiler over the water simmering in the bottom and, while stirring the egg mixture constantly with a wooden spoon or heat-proof rubber spatula, return the water in the bottom to a boil. Heat the egg mixture until the butter melts and the mixture feels hot to a fingertip, about 5 minutes.
8. Remove the egg mixture from the heat, and add the flour mixture. Stir until smooth. Using the rubber spatula, stir in the vanilla extract and the cooled nuts. Stir in the butterscotch morsels.

9. Spoon the batter into the prepared pan, smoothing the top.
10. Bake for 25 to 28 minutes, or until the cake springs back a little when gently pressed in the center. Do not overbake. If you want a slightly gooey center, remove the pan at 25 minutes. Transfer the pan to a wire rack to cool—or slice and serve from the pan.
11. Serve warm or at room temperature.

This is an Inskeepian favorite.

As host of *Morning Edition*, in at 3:00 A.M. and knee-deep in updates to the show by the time I roll in about six hours later, Steve rarely has time to even dash off feedback about the sweet offerings left in his office by the overgrown former *Morning Edition* elf working at *ATC*. He inhales the sugar and keeps moving until noon. But every now and then, something stops him in his tracks and I get a note, a phone call, or an appearance above my cubicle wall by the red-haired man himself. That's what happened after I made these. I got a note immediately ("BUTTERSCOTCH!!!!!") followed by a phone call, which was interrupted by an update, and then a visit from Steve to the light side of the building (*Morning* is on the dark side, oddly enough) to see if any more bars were left over. You can't fake enthusiasm like that, especially if you've been up since three.

This recipe comes from the Internet site CDKitchen and serves 16.

Fried Pies

YOU'LL NEED

A food processor
A rolling pin
A biscuit cutter
A pastry brush
A deep fryer and a slotted metal spatula
Plenty of paper towels and a few paper plates

FOR THE PIE DOUGH

One 8-ounce package cold cream cheese, cut into 8 pieces
2 sticks (1 cup) cold butter, cut into 8 pieces
2 cups all-purpose flour (see Tip)
½ teaspoon salt

FOR THE FILLING

Your choice of Fried Pie Filling (page 147, but see Tip)

FOR FINISHING THE PIES

1 large egg
1 teaspoon water
Safflower oil for frying OR 4 tablespoons unsalted butter, melted, for baking
Coarse or confectioners' sugar for dusting

Tips: In an attempt to make Fried Pies a TAD healthier, I sometimes use 1 cup of all-purpose flour and 1 cup of whole wheat flour. The dough has a nuttier taste, but it's still good.

Instead of making one of the fillings on page 147, feel free to use a canned pie filling, preferably cherry, lemon, or chocolate. This is one recipe I don't mind cheating on.

TO MAKE THE PIE DOUGH

1. Let the cream cheese and butter rest for 10 minutes at room temperature.
2. In a food processor, combine the flour and salt, then drop cut-up pieces of cream cheese and butter over the top. Pulse 6 to 10 times, stopping to scrape down the sides of the bowl, until the dough forms large curds.
3. Take the dough out and divide into 4 discs. Wrap in plastic and refrigerate for at least 2 hours before rolling out.
4. Meanwhile, make one of the fillings.
5. On a floured work surface, roll out the cold dough to a thickness of ¼ inch. Begin in the center of the disc, and flour the rolling pin if the dough sticks.
6. With a biscuit cutter, cut out as many circles as you can. Flour them lightly so they don't stick together, and place them on a plate. Gather up the scraps of dough and set aside.

7. Reflour the work surface, roll out the second disc of dough, cut out more pastry circles, and set aside. Gather up the scraps of dough and combine them with the reserved scraps from the first disc. Gently knead the dough together into one disc, wrap, and pop into the refrigerator.
8. Roll out the third and fourth discs in the same manner, kneading the excess dough into a disc and refrigerating.

CONTINUED –

Here's the thing that is so cool about being from a fairly homogeneous hometown and working at NPR: You really learn a lot about people from other regions, other traditions, and other countries, and occasionally they get to learn from you. For a brief moment you realize, "Hey, I'm not as boring and white bread as I thought!"

Back in March of 2006, I came across a series of reports in the *Atlanta Journal Constitution* chronicling the plight of Willie Watts, a sixty-something home baker who supplemented her monthly income by making Fried Pies and selling them at a barbecue place in Lithonia, Georgia. Mr. Watts had health problems, and what the missus earned paid for his medications, plus making Fried Pies was just something she liked to do. Well, the *AJC* reported her story, which had an unfortunate consequence: The Georgia Department of Agriculture, which regulates food prep and sales, shut her down because she was working from an unregulated kitchen. Fortunately, she was able to work out of the barbecue's kitchen in Lithonia, and her plight caught the eyes of a number of state representatives, who attempted to pass an exemption law that would allow her to return to her home kitchen. I pitched this story at *ATC*'s morning meeting, and Melissa Block interviewed Mrs. Watts about her Fried Pie operation that afternoon.

Nobody in the morning meeting had ever had a Fried Pie. To me, it was like saying you'd never written with a number-2 pencil. Fried Pies are small, crescent-shaped doughy pods filled with apples, cherries, sweet potatoes, lemon, or chocolate. They're generally cooked in melted shortening, then powdered with sugar or glazed with icing. We used to get them at local fairs or the Tastee-Freez in Virginia when I was a kid. They were more readily available when I moved to Georgia. Say "Fried Pie" to my cake-hating Georgia husband, and he'll offer to clean the bathrooms, prune the red tips hedges out front, vacuum the rugs, reorganize the attic, anything so I can fry some up. And he'll eat about twelve in one sitting.

After Melissa B. talked with Willie W., the whole *ATC* staff was dying of culinary curiosity. I went online to see if there was a way to order Fried Pies and have them delivered, only to discover yet again what a lame town DC is for Southern food. Then I decided to figure it out on my own, based on Mrs. Watts's description of her pie-making process.

Well, my Fried Pies (pictured on page 132) are still evolving and getting better all the time. When a few of our producers go to Baghdad, I bake whatever they want before they go, and then repeat it when they get back eight weeks later. Several of them have had Fried Pies coming and going. And no matter how many incredible cakes I bring in week after week, the inevitable question always comes up: "Hey! When are we getting Fried Pies again?"

Sadly, attempts by the Georgia legislature to get Mrs. Watts that exemption didn't work that session; it was among several last-minute changes that didn't get finalized as the assembly wound down. Last I heard, she was still working out of the barbecue place in Lithonia.

Fried Pies are best served immediately. They get greasy just hanging around too long. I've tried coating them in butter and baking them, which keeps the crust flakey. These are Faux Fried Pies, and only I know the difference.

I use Dorie Greenspan's rugelach dough recipe for the dough, but any regular pie dough recipe works fine, so long as it's fairly flexible and forgiving.

This should be enough to make about 18 Fried Pies.

Fried Pies — CONTINUED

9. Roll out the discs of dough scraps, cut out the pastry circles, and combine the scraps. Again, knead together the scraps, but this time continue rolling out the dough and cutting circles until there's just a finger length of dough left. Set that little piece aside to test the oil when you're ready to fry.

10. Clear the work surface of any sticky dough and reflour. Roll out the biscuit shapes to ⅛ inch thickness. Lightly flour and collect them on a plate until all the pastry rounds are now thin minipancakes.

TO FILL THE PIES

11. Whisk together the egg and water. Set aside along with a pastry brush and fork.

12. Clear the work surface and lay out as many pastry circles as you can. Get your filling.

13. Drop 1 heaping tablespoon of filling, but no more, on ONE HALF of each circle. DO NOT SPREAD.

14. Take the pastry brush and brush the egg mixture around the edges of the half circle where the filling is. Then fold over the empty half, forming a half-moon or pod. Using a fork, gently press down on the edge. Set the pie aside. Repeat until all the pastry circles are filled, painted with egg wash, folded, and forked.

TO FRY THE PIES

15. Fill your deep fryer with at least 2 inches of oil and turn it on. Use a pinch of the leftover dough to test when the oil is ready. The dough will puff and fry up to a golden brown in about a minute. Remove from the oil.

16. Using a slotted spatula, place as many pies as will float on the surface of your deep fryer.

17. Keep a watchful eye and flip the pies over when the bottoms are golden brown. Using the slotted spatula, remove from the fryer when the second side is done. Drain over the oil, then place the pies on paper towels to drain some more. Allow the pies to cool completely.

OR, TO BAKE THE PIES

15. Center a rack and preheat the oven to 350 degrees F. Spray a shallow baking pan with baking spray.

16. Use a pastry brush, coat both sides of each pie with some of the melted butter.

17. Arrange the pies evenly in the prepared pan. Bake for 10 minutes, remove from the oven, flip the pies over, then bake for 10 minutes more, until golden brown.

TO FINISH THE PIES

18. Dust the cooled pies with sugar and dig in.

A Trio of Fried Pie Fillings SEVERAL OPTIONS HERE.

Apple

YOU'LL NEED
A double boiler, real or improvised

2 Granny Smith apples
1 Gala, Braeburn, or Fuji apple
¼ cup brown sugar
½ teaspoon ground cinnamon
¼ teaspoon ground nutmeg
Pinch of salt
½ cup water

1. Peel, core, and dice the apples and toss with the brown sugar, cinnamon, nutmeg, and salt.
2. Pour about 1 inch of water in the bottom of a double boiler and put the apple mixture in the top. Place over medium-high heat, add the water to the apples, and stir. Stew until the mixture is tender and thick. Add extra spices and sugar to your taste.

Blueberry

YOU'LL NEED
A double boiler, real or improvised

¾ cup blueberries
¾ cup sugar
½ cup water

1. Pour about 1 inch of water in the bottom of a double boiler and combine the blueberries, sugar, and ½ cup of water in the top.
2. Stew over medium heat until the mixture is tender and thick.

Sweet Potato

YOU'LL NEED
1 medium sweet potato
1 tablespoon butter
½ teaspoon ground cinnamon
½ teaspoon ground nutmeg

1. Bake the sweet potato until done (see step 1 on page 46).
2. Remove the skin. In a large bowl, mash the sweet potato with the butter, cinnamon, and nutmeg. If you're also making apple filling, you can add 2 tablespoons of that. Mash together.

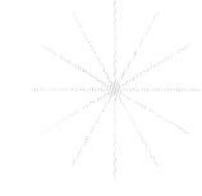

Chapter Four

LAYER CAKES, ANGEL FOOD CAKES, MODERATELY SINFUL CAKES, ALL ON THE ROAD TO HEAVEN AND HELL

WELCOME TO THE FANCY-PANTS ZONE!

Hard hat required

PEOPLE LOVE FROSTED LAYER CAKES, LOVE THEM. THIS IS PERHAPS BECAUSE THEY DO NOT HAVE TO MAKE THEM, MAKE THEM.

There has to be a special occasion for me to even consider baking a cake from this collection. It's not that I don't LOVE frosted layer cakes; if one magically appeared on my desk during a particularly hard day at work, I would have to fight the urge to bury my face in said cake for the sole purpose of eating my way out. No, it's the time involved in constructing these fancy-pants cakes that give me pause. Let me explain:

First, the batter: Making the batter is in itself not horribly time consuming. But I have a wee oven, so if I want to make a multilayer cake right, it takes twice as long, because I can only fit two round cake pans in the wee oven at a time. A task that should take 40 minutes takes 1 hour and 20 minutes.

Second, frosting the cake: This in itself is not horribly time consuming, either. But I have noticed that frosted cake recipes NEVER give you the right amount of frosting, so inevitably I end up making frosting TWICE. Occasionally, this means I have to make a second trip to the store. When things go well, this takes 15 minutes. When they go not-so-well, this takes 45 minutes.

Third, constructing the cake: This in itself is not horribly time consuming, but it can be a disaster, especially if you didn't divide your layers right, or maybe you did and you accidentally broke one while transferring it from the rack to the cake plate. Or maybe you don't have enough frosting to even up the boo-boos. Putting the cake together can take between 20 and 30 minutes.

And don't forget to tally the time it takes for the cake to cool to room temperature before you begin frosting. When it all adds up, we're talking 4 hours minimum, 6 hours maximum, and one dour, sour Melissa.

All that being said, it IS important for any home baker worth her (or his) salt to know how to make a proper layer cake. There's going to be a birthday, not your own, sometime in the future, and you will be asked to create a chocolate layer cake, and you, out of pride, will not be able to turn down the request. I know. This happens to me all the blessed time.

Dour, sour, martyr Melissa.

There is no room in my kitchen for martyrs, so I will suck it up. The good news is I'll probably inhale some cake and frosting at the same time. Plus, just like any other endeavor, the more you practice, the sharper your skills become. I only tell you the bad stuff because we're very honest with each other, you and I. I wouldn't let you stick a fork in an electrical socket; nor would I lead you blissfully unwarned into what can be the most frustrating level of Kingdom Cakedom.

I don't mean to make fancy-pants cakes sound like the fourth circle of hell. They can actually be quite fun and the payoff for making them is high. And some of them have interesting histories as well.

By the way, if you haven't figured it out by now, the number of servings you get per cake depends on how you slice it. A typical layer cake will serve between 20 and 32 people. From here on, let's just keep those numbers in our heads unless a recipe says otherwise, um-kay?

And for those of us who LOVE TOOLS, well, these cakes give us a good excuse to go out and buy MORE TOOLS!

CAKE-MAKING ACCESSORIES!

At this point, if you have not bought a handheld mixer and a double boiler, now is the time to do so. Many frostings require you to beat them in a saucepan over simmering water. If you have not bought at least 2 round cake pans of the exact same dimension (9 inches in diameter is the standard), now is the time. If you do not own at least a mini-food processor, now is the time to invest (actually, I'd suggest a larger one, if you've got the kitchen space). If you have not bought parchment paper, now is the time. If your spatula has become kind of ratty, get a new one. And while you're at the store, pick up a candy thermometer, too. If you don't have a long bread knife, consider getting one. And pick up some toothpicks and a wee plastic ruler; this is for evening up and dividing your cake layers. Better yet, consider investing in a Wilton cake layer cutter: it's adjustable and fairly easy to use and is generally found in any arts and crafts store that carries cake decorating utensils and equipment.

Making it PRETTY

I'm not going to get really detailed about the Many and Wondrous Ways to Pimp Your Cake. That's for another book, by another author. I'm too impatient; I want to eat my cake, not try out for a VH1 reality show. If you want to pipe glorious designs in icing, feel free to pick up one of those cake decorating kits and find a book to go with it. Like colored icing? Pick up some food dye, too.

Coming up: the Lane Cake (page 193), which had a memorable cameo in Harper Lee's novel *To Kill a Mockingbird*; Dark-Chocolate Red Velvet Cake (page 177), for which I've written a special ditty; plus bridging the divide between coconut lovers and coconut haters (page 167). All these cakes have survived the discriminating palates of the NPR staff, including our first cake, which is requested over and over again: Poor Niece Melissa's Attempt to Re-create Aunt Di's Bittersweet-Chocolate Frosted Layer Cake (page 157). Pay close attention; it covers the very basics of baking and frosting a layer cake, information you'll need for the rest of this chapter.

But first, a story.

MY AUNT DI

Doris Calvary Ambrose Moore was my maternal grandmother's sister, the eldest of four girls, raised during the Depression by a mother who could not read or write. Later, when Aunt Di (who, of course is actually my great-aunt) learned how to bake, it was always "a pinch of this, a bit of that, fill this bowl halfway with that and add a half a can of this, and mix until it tastes right." When my Grandma Marshall (technically, Great-Grandma Marshall) got older (and she was only sixteen years older than her firstborn), Aunt Di would help her make the Christmas cakes. This was back before everybody had electric mixers, so Aunt Di brought her fearsome forearms to the task. By the time Christmas Day rolled around, they'd have tin upon tin of cakes at the ready: fruitcakes, coconut cakes, pound cakes, and chocolate frosted layer cakes.

When I was growing up (this would have been the Ford-Carter-Reagan years) we'd spend part of Christmas Day visiting Momma's family: her sister, parents, Grandma Marshall, Aunt Di, and Uncle Alec. All of them very conveniently lived within walking distance of each other. They all had cake, too, and you could not refuse a slice. Fortunately, you COULD request they wrap it up in tinfoil so you could eat it later. Aunt Di's was the only place where we'd actually eat a slice AND take some of it home. Her bittersweet-chocolate frosted layer cake was too good not to have seconds, especially since it only came around once a year.

Aunt Di was such a hoot. I remember being introduced to the concept of free association in psychology class, which basically meant talking about whatever popped into your head. I hardly needed an introduction: I'd been listening to Aunt Di talk like this my whole life. Her conversation on Christmas Day went something like this:

"Oh, dahlin', so good to see you, how are you doin', did you hear about Donald Sutton? Lord, child, he's some kinda sick. Virgie called and said they had to take him over to Riverside Hospital last night and I know they are all worried, here, have yourself a slice of chocolate cake, dahlin'. You want some co-cola? Here, have some co-cola with that. Did you see all my cards in yonder? I need to show you the pictures Goldie sent me. You want another piece of cake, dahlin'? Here, take some home to your Daddy, they say Donald Sutton started feeling poorly just a few weeks ago . . ."

She was always quick, with a memory like a steel trap, and it was sad to see her slowing down. I'd started the Cake Project the year she turned ninety, and try as we might, none of us could nudge Aunt Di into giving us the recipe for her cake. It's not that she didn't want to share it; the recipe was locked into her manual memory. Aunt Di had done it for so long, without ever writing it down, that she couldn't remember unless she was in the process of making it herself, and she'd become too frail to attempt that.

The first Christmas without her, I decided to try to re-create the bittersweet-chocolate frosted layer cake. I came very close. I was helped by a World War II–era recipe and a new product put out by Hershey's: Special Dark Cocoa. And trite as it sounds, even though it's not exactly her cake, and even though I usually don't like making layer cakes, whenever I make this recipe, I think of Aunt Di, and it's truly a labor of love.

POOR NIECE MELISSA'S HUMBLE ATTEMPT AT RE-CREATING

Aunt Di's Bittersweet-Chocolate Frosted Layer Cake

NEW TECHNIQUE ALERT!

UNMOLDING AND DIVIDING LAYERS, FROSTING LAYER CAKES

YOU'LL NEED

A whisk attachment for mixer
Three 8-inch round or two 9-inch round cake pans
3 medium mixing bowls

FOR THE CAKE

2 cups sugar
3 cups cake flour
½ teaspoon salt
4 teaspoons baking powder
4 large eggs
2 cups heavy whipping cream
2 teaspoons vanilla extract

FOR THE FROSTING (SEE TIP)

1 stick (½ cup) unsalted butter
1 cup Hershey's Special Dark Cocoa
4 cups confectioners' sugar
⅔ cup milk
1½ teaspoons vanilla extract

Tip: This recipe makes enough frosting for two 9-inch layers or three 8-inch ones. BUT, you can make more layers by cutting the baked layers in half horizontally (see page 159). If you do, double the recipe for the frosting.

TO MAKE THE CAKE

1. Place your mixer bowl and wire whisk attachment in the freezer. This will help when you're whipping the cream in a few minutes.
2. Center a rack and preheat the oven to 350 degrees F.
3. To make it easy to unmold the cakes, use parchment paper to line the bottoms of those pans, and spray the sides with baking spray. (Dorie Greenspan calls this the "belt AND suspenders" method of greasing!)
4. In one bowl, measure out your sugar. In a second bowl, dry whisk your flour, salt, and baking powder together. In a third bowl, beat your eggs with a handheld mixer until thick.

CONTINUED –

Like I said, we have no idea how Aunt Di made her cake. I tried a basic yellow butter cake, but it wasn't quite right. And then one day I saw an article in the *Washington Post* about this whipped cream cake. Not whipped cream like you get in the frozen food section; this is the heavy whipping cream you find in the dairy section, and you whip it yourself. You whip it good.

I say, "Whip it!"

Sorry. I just had a Devo moment. Anyway, the recipe comes from *The American Woman's Cook Book*, which was popular during the early to middle years of the twentieth century.

The crumb, according to my Mom, is fluffier and more delicate than Aunt Di's because I use cake flour (she always used all-purpose), but the taste is dead-on.

As for the bittersweet-chocolate frosting, that's still a work in progress. We know Aunt Di used cocoa, milk, butter, vanilla extract, and confectioners' sugar for the frosting. We don't know how much of each ingredient. I've got the taste right, but not the thick, fudgy consistency with that hardened outer shell, though I think it's just a matter of time before I nail that.

What I've come up with in the meantime is good enough to rate as Melissa Block's Number 1 Favorite Cake. If I don't make one every few months or so, she's sure to drop a couple of hints. Or she nudges other people to drop hints. She's crazy persistent that way.

This cake can serve 16 to 24.

Aunt Di's Bittersweet-Chocolate Frosted Layer Cake – CONTINUED

5. OK, by this time, your mixing bowl and whisk attachment should be nice and cold. Remove them from the freezer and assemble on your mixer. Add the cream to the bowl and whip on medium-high to high speed until the cream holds its shape—basically, until it's as thick as Cool Whip or softened ice cream. This should take 2 to 3 minutes.
6. Slow the mixer down to medium and add the beaten eggs. Return to medium-high speed and whip (I say whip it!) until the mixture is slightly foamy.
7. Slow the mixer down to medium and gradually add the sugar and then the vanilla extract.
8. Stop the mixer. Remove your whisk attachment and attach your regular paddle or beaters. Use a spatula to scrape down the sides of the bowl.
9. With the mixer on medium speed, gradually add the flour mixture.
10. Pour the batter into the prepared pans. OK. This part always drives me catnip crazy. Your goal is to bake 2 or 3 equal layers. You do that by dividing the batter equally among your cake pans. And I guarantee you'll never get it absolutely perfect.

    Some bakers use a kitchen scale. Others eyeball it, counting out spoonfuls. Still others use their plastic rulers and measure on the inside of the pan, running their finger or a brush through the floured-baking spray coating before pouring the batter to create a pour line.

    I'll say it again—you're never going to get the layers absolutely equal.

    Which is why I've quit aiming for equality. Each cake layer is going to have a slight dome shape to it anyway. This is why I have a long bread knife: to even up the layers.
11. Place the pans on the same rack toward the center of the oven, but don't let them touch.

    OK. This part drives me catnip crazy, too. As you know, I have a ridiculously small oven: there is no room for two 9-inch pans on one rack. BUT putting them on separate racks isn't ideal: they're not going to bake well if one is below the other. So I use two 8-inch pans on one rack together and plan on a 2- or 4-layer cake.
12. Bake for 20 to 25 minutes, until the cake pulls away from the sides of the pan. When you see this, gently pull the rack out of the oven partway and test the cake with a toothpick or skewer. When it comes out clean, remove from the oven and let cool for 10 minutes in the pans. While the layers are baking or cooling . . .

TO MAKE THE FROSTING

13. Fit the mixer with clean beaters or a paddle. Melt the butter in the microwave or in a saucepan over low heat. Pour the butter into the mixing bowl and add the cocoa. Mix on medium-low speed until smooth. Gradually add the confectioners' sugar, alternating with the milk. Mix until smooth. Add the vanilla extract and mix until incorporated. Set aside.

TO FINISH THE CAKE

14. Unmold the cake layers.

NEW TECHNIQUE

UNMOLDING AND DIVIDING THE LAYERS

Before unmolding the cakes, get a sheet of parchment paper and a plate, then take a look at the tops of your cakes. One is going to look slightly more even than the other. That's the one you want for the top layer, the crown.

Place the parchment over that cake pan, put the plate over the cake pan, then flip. Remove the pan and peel off the old parchment paper that once lined the cake pan. Put your plate upside down on the bottom of the flipped cake, then flip again. Remove the plate and the fresh parchment paper. Your cake crown will now be right side up.

For the second layer, put the plate upside down on top of the cake pan and flip. Remove the old parchment paper. Allow both layers to cool completely.

Now, you could have a cake with just 2 or 3 fat layers, and that would be fine. But if you love frosting (like my Aunt Di did), you'll want to have more layers. The way to do that is to cut each layer in half horizontally (Quick! Do the math!) Yes, that's 4 or 6 layers. Aunt Di usually had anywhere from 5 to 8, depending on how things went the week before Christmas. She often doubled the recipe.

There are a number of techniques for dividing your layers.

OLD SCHOOL: Using your plastic ruler, measure the height of each layer and figure out where the middle is. So if your layer is $1\frac{1}{2}$ inches tall, the midpoint would be $\frac{3}{4}$ inch from the bottom or top. Then, imagine the cake is your head and you're sticking your index fingers in your ears, and stick two toothpicks into opposite sides of the cake at the midpoint. Now pretend that cake layer is a clock, with those two toothpicks at 12 and 6 o'clock. Put toothpicks at 2, 4, 8, and 10 o'clock. And now, using the toothpicks as guides, use a large bread knife to divide your layer in half, gently sawing back and forth until you've divided the layer in half.

CONTINUED —

Aunt Di's Bittersweet-Chocolate Frosted Layer Cake — CONTINUED

NEW SCHOOL: Determine the midpoint of each layer as described above. Then adjust your Wilton cake cutter to the appropriate measurement. Steady the cake with one hand and, with the cake cutter in the other, use a gentle back-'n'-forth sawing motion to divide the layer. Depending on how tender your cake crumb is, you might have to start the dividing cut with a bread knife before switching to the cake cutter. Be gentle when finishing the cut, too; you don't want a chunk of cake to come off the back end.

Now, there's the DENTAL SCHOOL method involving dental floss, but I've never mastered it. Do like the NPR staff do and Google if you're curious. But my money's on the Wilton cake cutter.

After dividing your layers, use a bread knife and another big knife (a cleaver works well) to lift and transport the top half of the layer to a rack or plate. This is easy: you're going to use the flat side of two knife blades like a forklift.

First, pretend you're using your knife to cut horizontally, but instead, gently position each knife about 2 inches left and right from the center of the cake. Simply lift up the already divided top layer with the knives and place it on a plate, with the knives still in position. After you've frosted the bottom layer, use the knives again like a forklift to reposition the top half of the layer in place.

15. Frost the cake.

NEW TECHNIQUE

FROSTING A LAYER CAKE

Survey your layers. Simple rule: best one goes on top, worst one on bottom, the rest in the middle.

I have found through trial and error that it is a hell of a lot easier to put frosting on the browned part of the cake layers than the raw crumb. So generally I will put each layer raw-crumb-side down. This is contradictory to what they tell you in the "how to frost a cake" directions of some cookbooks. But it works for me.

So does "priming" the cake. When you paint walls or a canvas, you usually apply primer, a thin, usually white, layer of paint. To prime the top and sides of your cake, simply apply a thin layer of frosting, refrigerate for 10 minutes, then apply a second, thicker layer.

To keep your serving plate clean while you frost the cake, cut four 1-inch strips of wax or parchment paper and arrange them in a square on the plate so that the edges of the first layer will be on the paper.

Transfer your worst layer, raw-crumb-side down, to the plate.

Using a large spatula, spoon frosting onto the center of the cake. Spread out the frosting to make a thin layer rotating the plate as you go, and trying to keep the frosting smooth and even. Make sure to always work from the center of the cake outward, and to take the frosting all the way to the edge of the layer.

Transfer your next layer, raw-crumb-side down, on top of the frosted layer and frost its top as described above.

Continue like this until you've crowned the cake with the best-looking top layer. Frost the top.

Now, to do the sides of the cake, it's helpful to raise the cake so it's at about your chest level. There are special cake spinners you can buy for this, and you might want to invest in one if you find that frosting cakes is your passion. I just flip my big mixing bowl over (it has a wide base) and balance the cake plate on top.

When I've got my Martha Stewart Perfectionista hat on, I take a butter knife and scrape loose crumbs off the sides before applying a thin layer of frosting. I find that it's easier to frost the sides of the cake with a small spatula, starting at about 1/2 inch from the bottom with a medium-size dollop of frosting, working my way UP the sides of the cake. I do one complete rotation, then carefully fill in the gap, starting with a small dollop of frosting 1/2 inch from the bottom. After that's done, I wipe off the spatula, then use it to add more frosting or to smooth or texture the sides of the cake.

Smoothing is easy—you just try to even out the sides and top of the cake as best you can. But smooth is also boring. If I've spent 4 hours slaving over this sweet monstrosity, I want the frosting to bear the mark of the maker. So I purposely make waves in the frosting with the spatula. Sometimes I use long, straight strokes; sometimes I go Van Gogh and use undulating *Starry Night* strokes; and sometimes I go telegraph and use short strokes and dashes—depends on my mood.

After frosting, I generally let the cake set for 15 to 20 minutes before removing the wax strips underneath. This allows the frosting to harden slightly. To remove the wax strips, hold both sides taut and ease the strip toward you. Take a folded wet paper towel and use the edges to clean any stray frosting on the plate.

16. Serve or cover for later.

Whipped Cream **Cake**

YOU'LL NEED

Two 8-inch round cake pans

1 cup whipping cream
2 eggs, beaten until thick and lemon colored
1 cup sugar
1 teaspoon vanilla
1½ cups sifted cake flour
¼ teaspoon salt
2 teaspoons baking powder
Seven-Minute Icing (recipe follows)

Whip cream until it holds its shape. Add eggs and whip until light as foam. Add sugar and beat again. Add vanilla. Sift flour, salt, and baking powder together 3 times and add to egg mixture. Bake in greased layer cake pans in a moderate oven (350 degrees F) 25 to 30 minutes. Makes two 8-inch layers. Cool and spread Seven-Minute Icing or whipped cream between the layers and on top.

Seven-Minute Icing

This is slightly different from the Seven-Minute Frosting on page 80.

YOU'LL NEED

1 unbeaten egg white
⅞ cup granulated sugar
3 tablespoons cold water
½ teaspoon flavor extract

Place all the ingredients in the top of a double boiler. Place over boiling water and beat with beater for 7 minutes. Add flavorings, beat, and spread on the cake.

FLAVORING OPTIONS

1. Chocolate: Add to above one and ½ ounces melted, unsweetened chocolate two minutes before taking from fire.

Melissa's Note: Yeah, it took me a minute or two to figure the chocolate directions, too. Here's the translation: Add 1½ ounces of melted unsweetened chocolate 5 minutes into beating the icing. Beat for 2 more minutes.

2. Coffee: Use cold boiled coffee in place of water.

Melissa's Note: Coffee? That means one thing—PEDICURE TIME! Let's all run to Starbucks then go to the nail place next door! I'll take the *Glamour* magazine and you take *Cosmopolitan*! Maybe between the two of us, we'll finally find out "What Women REALLY want!"

3. Vanilla: Now, Debra Bruno's grandmother used 1/2 teaspoon of vanilla extract for flavoring, so there's another option for you.

Let's get back to *The American Woman's Cook Book* (see page 157). I first learned about it from the food section of the *Washington Post* in an article by Debra Bruno, "The Cake Through Which I Came to Know My Grandmother." She wrote about her grandmother's copy of *The American Woman's Cook Book*, especially about the notations throughout: "There is a detailed record of her cooking triumphs: 18 markings of 'excellent,' 19 with 'swell,' 4 'delicious,' 1 'good' and 1 'very, very good' painstakingly written along with month, day, and year from 1946 to 1979."

Debra went on to say that she was able to glimpse fragments of her family history, including the Whipped Cream Cake made on March 10, 1946, her mother's fifteenth birthday.

The cake became a Cake Project recipe of the week. I made it, and it was "excellent, swell" and then some. Light and fluffy—the perfect white frosted cake!

Jimmy managed to track down a used copy of the cookbook for me—it's the size of a medium hardcover dictionary, with a green, well-worn, stained cover and this mysterious inscription on the front plate:

Eve—
You can live without poetry, music and art,
You can live without movies, with a broken heart,
You can live without friends and live without books,
But civilized man cannot live without cooks!

—The Coppers. Christmas, 1943.

I swear, I don't know Eve from Adam, but I want that on my headstone.

Again, this is the same cake as Aunt Di's Bittersweet-Chocolate Frosted Layer Cake (page 157). But Aunt Di's is a doubled recipe of this cake. And this one has a different frosting. If you're feeling unsure, turn to the directions for Aunt Di's cake. At left are the original instructions for the cake as they appear in the book. Be forewarned: it's a small cake, and serves 12 to 16 people.

Honey Buttercream and Apricot Jam Cake

ANOTHER OPTION FOR THE WHIPPED CREAM CAKE

YOU'LL NEED

Two 8-inch or 9-inch round cake pans
A whisk attachment and extra bowl for mixer
A double boiler, real or improvised
A hand-held mixer

Double recipe Whipped Cream Cake (page 162) *without* frosting (see Tip)
1 cup sugar
4 large egg whites
3 sticks (1½ cups) unsalted butter, cut into pats, at room temperature
¼ cup fresh lemon juice (from 2 large lemons)
1 teaspoon vanilla extract
1½ teaspoons honey
⅔ cup good-quality apricot jam, slightly warmed or stirred until spreadable

Tip: This is the same as the recipe of Aunt Di's Bittersweet-Chocolate Frosted Layer Cake, page 157, again without the frosting. The instructions in the Aunt Di cake are modern and already doubled for you, while those for the Whipped Cream Cake are from the 1940s, so I suggest you go with the Aunt Di cake.

TO MAKE THE CAKE AND FROSTING

1. Make the cake layers, following the instructions for the Whipped Cream Cake (or, better, Aunt Di's).
2. While the cake is cooling, make the frosting. In the top of a double boiler over simmering water, whisk together the sugar and egg whites for 3 minutes. The mixture will look like shiny marshmallow cream. Remove from the heat.
3. Using a handheld mixer on medium speed, beat until the meringue has cooled, about 5 minutes.
4. Add the butter pats, a third at a time, beating until smooth.
5. Beat the buttercream on medium-high speed for 6 to 10 minutes, until it is thick and very smooth. If the buttercream curdles or separates, just keep beating. It will come together.
6. Lower the speed to medium, and gradually beat in the lemon juice, then the vanilla extract and honey. You should have a smooth buttercream. Cover tightly with plastic and set aside.

TO CONSTRUCT THE CAKE

7. Following the instructions on page 159, divide each cooled layer in half, and separate the halves so that you have 4 layers.

8. Place the bottom layer on the cake plate. Spread a thin layer of buttercream on the top, spreading it out from the center. Next spread a thin layer of apricot jam on top of the frosting. Add the next cake layer and repeat until you reach the crown.

9. Frost the top of the crown with buttercream. Scrape away any excess jam from the side and then frost the sides of the cake.

All I can say is, "Thank you, Lord, for Dorie Greenspan!" Whenever I have a cake conundrum, I e-mail Dorie for encouragement and she always comes through.

I was hankering for buttercream frosting one day, so I pulled out one of my Baking Perfectionista cookbooks and came across a buttercream recipe involving egg yolks. Game, as always, for any kitchen adventure involving sweets, I followed the directions to a *T*. Disaster. The fats in the butter seemed to be separating, and nothing I did could convince them to rejoin in holy dairy-mony.

I tried the recipe again, thinking maybe I'd been abducted by aliens during the last go-round, thus skipping an important step. *Disaster*, the sequel. The buttercream tasted right, but it wasn't doing right. I put it in the refrigerator, hoping to firm the mix up. When I was ready to frost, I gently whisked the cooled buttercream, and it laughed at me. I frosted the cake anyway, stored it in the refrigerator overnight, and took it into work on Monday. It looked like it was melting.

The whole experience made me advocate a violation of the number-1 Cake Project tenet: no store-bought mixes or frostings.

From: Melissa Gray
To: ATC staff
Subject: Today's Cake

I impart to you this life lesson: No matter how much leisure time you may have, life is too freakin' short for frosting that features more than 3 steps and takes as long as 3 hours.

Grab your keys. Leave your house. Go to the store. Buy the Betty Crocker buttercream. And know that you're not less of a baker for doing it.

Fortunately, part of my duties that week included a confab with Dorie about an upcoming baking segment for the show. I mentioned my buttercream fiasco. "Oh, no. That sounds like you tried to make Swiss buttercream. It's really way too much. There's an easier way. Don't give up." She pointed me toward the frosting in her Perfect Party Cake recipe, in her book *Baking: From My Home to Yours*. I tried it, and *voilà! wunderbar! whoohoo!* Buttercream just the way I like it!

Dorie's recipe also suggested spreading jam between layers for festive cakes. "That's SWELL!" I thought to myself, à la Debra Bruno's grandmother. I could see all kinds of possibilities for a buttercream frosted layer cake. I added honey to Dorie's buttercream, bought some high-quality apricot preserves, and had another workplace hit on my hands. Marrying the lightness of Whipped Cream Cake with the silkiness of buttercream and the sweetness of the apricots, this cake (pictured on page 148) makes an elegant dessert for springtime parties or get-togethers. Expect to serve 16 to 24.

with out

COCONUT/ NOT COCONUT CAKE

A COMPROMISE OF CONGRESSIONAL PROPORTIONS

Remember the good ol' days when the GOP and the Democrats used to compromise on legislation? I don't. But our political editor Ron Elving tells me it used to happen. I think it was during the years when my father walked backward barefoot in the snow to school every day and money grew on trees.

When you make a coconut cake, then take it into work, you are going to find you've instantly polarized your office. There are Haters who absolutely can't stand the stuff and Lovers who can't get enough of it. They do not communicate well with each other. Each side thinks the other is crazy. Each wants Monday cake. Neither will be fully satisfied. If they could, they would hold separate press conferences, trying to convince the American public that only theirs is the right, just, and reasonable position.

I have made delicious coconut cakes with coconut in the batter and coconut in the frosting and have suffered through entire days of whining from the Haters. Honestly, people I haven't seen in years walked down just to complain that I'd brought in a coconut cake and they hate coconut cake and why didn't I do chocolate instead? I have issued moratoriums on coconut cake, and then had to listen to weeks of whining from the Lovers. I have brought in cakes that contained coconut, but did not feature it as the dominant flavor (like Paula Deen's Grandgirl's Fresh Apple Cake, page 122) but that wasn't enough for them. They wanted a real coconut cake.

So, here's my simple solution: I bake a doubled recipe of Whipped Cream Cake (page 162).

I make a doubled recipe of its Seven-Minute Icing.

Using a spatula, I press coconut into the frosting on exactly HALF of each layer as I construct the cake. For consistency, I press it into the LEFT half of each layer. I add a tiny bit of extra frosting to the RIGHT side to keep the cake level before I add the next layer. I press coconut on the LEFT side of the frosted crown, and then I press coconut on the LEFT side of the cake.

I write a sign. It has arrows. One arrow points to the LEFT. It says "Coconut." One arrow points to the RIGHT. It says "NOT Coconut." I leave the cake up front with the sign and a knife and let both sides fight it out.

If only Capitol Hill worked the same way, maybe we'd all get a slice. Or have fewer politicians.

Alma's Italian **Cream Cake** YES, IT'S GOT COCONUT IN IT! AND WALNUTS!

YOU'LL NEED

Two 8-inch or 9-inch round cake pans
Baking pan
A food processor
A whisk attachment and extra bowl for mixer

FOR THE CAKE

2 cups walnuts
1½ sticks (¾ cup) unsalted butter, at room temperature
2 cups sugar
5 large eggs, separated
2 cups cake flour
1 teaspoon baking soda
½ teaspoon salt
1 cup buttermilk
1 teaspoon vanilla extract
1 cup sweetened shredded coconut

FOR THE FROSTING

One 8-ounce package cream cheese, at room temperature
1 stick (½ cup) butter, at room temperature
1 tablespoon vanilla extract
One 16-ounce box confectioners' sugar (about 3¾ cups)

TO MAKE THE CAKE

1. Center a rack and preheat the oven to 350 degrees F. Prepare the cake pans.
2. Spread out the walnuts in a shallow baking pan and toast them in the oven for 3 to 5 minutes. In a food processor, finely chop them until they resemble very coarse flour. Set aside 1 cup for the cake batter and reserve the remaining 1 cup for the frosting and for sprinkling on top of the cake.
3. Set aside ½ cup of sugar. Cream the butter in the mixer at medium speed, and gradually add the remaining 1½ cups of the sugar. Beat until light and fluffy. Add the egg yolks, one at a time, beating well after each addition.
4. In a separate bowl, dry whisk the flour, baking soda, and salt together.
5. Add the flour mixture to the creamed mixture, alternating with the buttermilk, 1 cup of flour mix for every ½ cup of buttermilk, beating well after each addition. Continue until all the flour and buttermilk are mixed in.
6. Add the vanilla extract, 1 cup of the chopped toasted walnuts, and the coconut and beat until well blended.
7. Set the batter aside while you beat the egg whites. Switch to a clean mixer bowl and replace the paddle or beaters with a whisk attachment.
8. Whip the egg whites on high speed until frothy, then continue whisking while gradually adding the remaining ½ cup of sugar. The egg whites should form stiff, but not dry, peaks.
9. Fold the egg whites into the batter in thirds, making sure each time that the egg whites are completely incorporated. All together, the folding will take between 10 and 15 full rotations of the bowl. Be gentle.
10. Pour the batter into the pans and bake for 30 to 35 minutes, until the cake layers test done.
11. Cool the layers in the pans for 10 minutes, then unmold onto cake racks. Allow to cool to room temperature.

TO MAKE THE FROSTING

12. Cream the cream cheese and butter together on medium speed and add the vanilla extract.
13. Gradually add the confectioners' sugar 1 cup at a time, until blended.
14. Kick up your mixer to high gear and beat the frosting until very smooth. Using a spatula or wooden spoon, stir in ½ cup of the reserved chopped walnuts. (You should have ½ cup left.)

CONSTRUCTING THE CAKE

15. Don't worry about separating the layers. Judging from Cat's beautiful cake photo, she likes great big undivided layers. Do level the top of the lower layer so that the layer stacks prettily. Frost the layers in the usual way, doing the sides last, after the crown.
16. THEN put cake in the refrigerator to firm up the frosting. About 30 minutes before serving, press the remaining ½ cup of chopped walnuts into the crown of the cake. Remember this "press chopped nuts into the frosting" trick for future cakes.

Working at NPR is a book lover's paradise. We are regularly inundated with all kinds of books because so many publishers want us to interview their authors. I think less than 5 percent of incoming books eventually make the cut—the leftovers get snapped up by our bibliophilic staff, who either read the books themselves or redistribute them to interested parties. What's left over gets donated to libraries or prisons.

The redistributors think I like books about Elvis, the South, shoes, and baking. And they would be right. I just wish they'd throw a little David McCullough or Malcolm Gladwell my way. As it is, I review what lands on my desk, set it aside for future consideration, or redistribute it myself.

That's how I came across this recipe. It's from Cat Cora's *Cooking from the Hip*. She's another one of those Food Network people, the star of *Iron Chef America*. Her book is about cooking fast meals. She has helpfully provided tips on how to convert leftovers to new dishes, and one day when I'm not living off of salad and cake, I may try a few more of these recipes because they look tasty. Alma's Italian Cream Cake certainly is. (Alma was Cat's grandmother, by the way.)

Sour Cream Spice Cake with Orange Butter Frosting

YOU'LL NEED

Two 8-inch or 9-inch round cake pans

FOR THE CAKE

2¼ cups sifted cake flour
¾ teaspoon baking soda
1 teaspoon baking powder
¼ teaspoon salt
2 teaspoons ground cinnamon
1 teaspoon ground nutmeg
½ teaspoon ground cloves
1⅔ cups sugar
2 sticks (1 cup) unsalted butter, melted and cooled
1 cup sour cream
3 large eggs
1 teaspoon vanilla extract

FOR THE FROSTING

1 stick (½ cup) unsalted butter, at room temperature
3 cups confectioners' sugar
¼ cup evaporated milk
1 teaspoon vanilla extract
1 teaspoon orange extract
3 tablespoons dried orange peel

TO MAKE THE CAKE

1. Center a rack and preheat the oven to 350 degrees F. Prepare the cake pans.
2. Dry whisk the flour, baking soda, baking powder, salt, cinnamon, nutmeg, and cloves together. Whisk in the sugar.
3. With the mixer on medium speed, beat together the melted and cooled butter, sour cream, eggs, and vanilla extract and continue beating on medium speed until thoroughly blended.
4. Gradually add the flour mixture and beat until thoroughly blended.
5. Pour the batter into the cake pans and bake for 25 to 30 minutes, until the cake layers test done.
6. Cool the layers in the pans for 10 minutes, then unmold onto cake racks and cool to room temperature.
7. Do not divide the layers, but do even up the top of the lower layer so that the layer stacks prettily.

TO MAKE THE FROSTING

8. Cream the butter in the mixer at medium speed. Beat in the confectioners' sugar, evaporated milk, vanilla extract, and orange extract. Mix until smooth. Add the orange peel and mix until incorporated.

9. Frost the cake and refrigerate for 20 minutes to firm up the frosting.

My neighbor Julie Sibbing brought me a 35-cent pamphlet with cake recipes after cleaning out her mother's cookbooks. It's a gift that just keeps on giving. The pamphlet is just forty-eight pages, with recipes so simplified that they might as well be haikus. It's called *200 Classic Cake Recipes*, and it was put together by the Culinary Arts Institute in 1969, the year I was born. "No complicated beating and mixing are necessary for this elegant Sour Cream Spice Cake," it proclaims. And it's true. There was only one problem: the *ATC* staff was split on the frosting. Some (my true Spice-and-Vicers) felt the crumb was so moist and good that it didn't need frosting, or should have only had a very thin layer. Others were completely gaga over the frosting and urged me to add MORE. With those two different reactions in mind, I think this cake works best with full, rather than divided, layers and a thin layer of frosting in between. For that reason, the frosting is enough for a 2-layer cake.

More CAKE LORE

It has been my experience that a Monday cake will be down to the last slice within an hour and a half of arriving at NPR. And then there's the long wait while that very last slice gets whittled down to half, and the half to a quarter, and then the quarter stands there, drying out. This drives me nuts. I never can catch the whittlers in the act, and though I've polled my co-workers, none will admit to it. As to why it happens, they suggest, "Well, maybe none of us wants to be the little piggy who eats the very last slice of cake."

Oh, so I assume there's nothing wrong with being the little piggy who eats the very first slice, or goes back for seconds or thirds? I need a human behaviorist here.

In the meantime, I need to get the cake plate and the carry cleaned before 1:00 P.M., when we start gearing up for our live 4:00 P.M. show. So I call my favorite cleanup hitter, Rob Ballenger, in Newscast. But even Rob is hesitant to finish off the last slice of layer cake that's sans frosting. This sounds barbaric, but it happens even at a place as civilized, smart, and classy as NPR: When the whittling begins, inevitably someone just lops off the frosting part.

I'm not going to name names, but this happened with comic brutality once. A veteran newsman was making his way out of the studio when he passed by the remaining hunk of a frosted spice cake, the equivalent of about three slices. Ignoring the cake knife, he used his BARE HANDS to tear off the top layer and toddled happily away. Our then-editor Quinn O'Toole saw the whole thing and couldn't stop laughing. "Quinn!" I said, aghast at a new low in office table manners. "Why didn't you stop him?"

"I was scared!" Quinn replied. "What if he took a swipe at me with his frosting-covered hands? Who'd edit the show?"

Now, whenever there's a frosted cake up front, one of the resident smarty-pants will joke about getting a slice early, before our cake scalper passes by.

Devil's Food Cake with Quick Fudge Icing and Raspberry Jam

IF YOU'RE GOING TO SIN, SIN BIG

YOU'LL NEED

Three 8-inch or two 9-inch round cake pans
2 medium bowls
A double-boiler, real or improvised

FOR THE CAKE

½ cup unsweetened cocoa
1 cup strong coffee, cooled
½ cup shortening
1½ cups sugar
2 large eggs
1 teaspoon vanilla extract
1½ cups cake flour
1 teaspoon baking soda
¾ teaspoon salt
½ teaspoon baking powder

FOR THE FROSTING AND FILLING

One 12-ounce package semisweet chocolate morsels
⅔ cup evaporated milk
2 cups confectioners' sugar
1 small jar good-quality raspberry jam, warmed or stirred vigorously

TO MAKE THE CAKE

1. Position a rack in the lower third of the oven and preheat to 350 degrees F. Prepare the cake pans.
2. In a bowl, whisk the cocoa and coffee until smooth. Set aside.

3. With the mixer on medium, combine the shortening and sugar, adding the sugar gradually. Add the eggs, one at a time, beating well after each addition. Add the vanilla extract.
4. In another bowl, dry whisk the flour, baking soda, salt, and baking powder together.

CONTINUED –

I have tried a number of basic chocolate cake recipes, and none of them satisfy quite like this one. The cake is from Stephen Pyles's Heaven and Hell Cake (page 209), which, incidentally, is the final and most challenging cake in this book.

(I know you just peeked. Yes, it's two cakes, plus a mousse and a chocolate ganache. Do not panic. You'll be more than prepared.)

Now, I rather dig devil's food cake with white frosting, and the Seven-Minute Icing on page 162 works fine, but eventually you'll have to satisfy your own Chocolate Cake Caucus. This combination will shut them up for a while. The crumb is richly chocolaty and moist, and a layer of raspberry jam gives the cake a fresh kick. The icing will smooth itself out and form a firm outer shell once it cools. Make sure to double it if you're baking more than 2 layers.

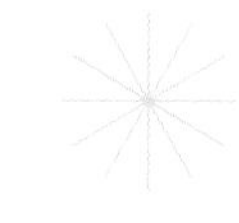

Devil's Food Cake with Quick Fudge Icing and Raspberry Jam — CONTINUED

5. Add half of the flour mixture to the creamed mixture, beat, then add the cocoa and coffee mixture and beat again. Add the remaining flour mixture and beat until smooth.

6. Pour the batter into the prepared cake pans and place on the oven rack as close to the middle as possible without touching. Bake for 30 minutes, or until the layers test done.

7. Cool the layers in the pans for 10 minutes, then unmold onto cake racks.

TO MAKE THE FROSTING

8. Melt the chocolate morsels with the evaporated milk in the top of a double boiler over simmering water, stirring constantly until fairly smooth. Remove from the heat.

9. Gradually add the sugar and beat with a wooden spoon or a handheld mixer until smooth. Set aside.

TO CONSTRUCT THE CAKE

10. Once the cake has cooled to room temperature, divide the layers if you wish (see page 159). Place the worst layer on the bottom, and save the best one for the top. If you do divide the layers, make sure the exposed crumb side faces down.

11. Place the bottom layer on the cake plate. Spread a layer of frosting on the top. Next spread a thin layer of raspberry jam on top of the frosting. Add the next cake layer and repeat until you reach the crown.

12. Frost the top of the crown. Scrape away any excess jam from the sides and then frost the sides of the cake.

Like, baking with chocolate: PART II

The Revenge of the Dutch Process Cocoa (DPC)

Sung to the theme from
The Beverly Hillbillies

Come and listen to a story 'bout a
    Red Velvet Cake
Made with Dutch process cocoa
Man, it tasted really great!
Only one problem
The cake it would not rise
Could not put it in this book, no
That would not be wise
Bad reviews you see—loss of face—no
credibility.

Well, the first thing I did was get a
    different brand
Of unsweetened cocoa
But that was really bland
So I added in some baking powder
And then some DPC
Then loaded up the mixer
It was fluffy as could be
Lots of air bubbles, that is
A springy, tasty cake
Ya'll come back now, ya hear?

O.K. Bernie Taupin (Elton John's lyricist) has nothing to fear. The lesson here is this: If you use Dutch process unsweetened cocoa in a cake recipe that doesn't include baking powder, you're going to get a flat, moist, dense—yet awfully tasty—cake. This goes back to our chemistry lesson on the reaction that makes cakes rise: the interaction between your leavening agent, moisture, and heat.

Regular unsweetened cocoa is acidic. The addition of baking soda, which is alkaline, reacts to that acidic property, enlarging all those air bubbles whipped into the batter during creaming, which when baked, result in a risen cake. Dutch process cocoa has an alkali already added to it to neutralize its acidic properties. It's like a big, heavy blanket over the bubble party. BUT, if you add baking powder, which has alkaline and acid properties that will react with each other when introduced to moisture and heat, well, party on, dude! Swimmin' pools! Movie stars!

Dark-Chocolate Red Velvet Cake

FOR THOSE FOR WHOM PLAIN RED VELVET CAKE IS TOO JEJUNE

YOU'LL NEED

Two 8-inch or 9-inch round cake pans
A food processor

FOR THE CAKE

2 sticks (1 cup) unsalted butter, at room temperature
1¼ cups sugar
1¼ cups light brown sugar
6 large eggs
2 teaspoons vanilla extract
3 cups all-purpose flour
¼ teaspoon baking soda
¼ cup Dutch process cocoa
½ teaspoon baking powder
1 cup sour cream
½ ounce red food coloring (half a 1-ounce standard bottle)

FOR THE FROSTING

½ cup (1 stick) unsalted butter, at room temperature
Two 8-ounce packages cream cheese, at room temperature
Two 16-ounce boxes confectioners' sugar (about 3¾ cups each)
1 teaspoon vanilla extract

CONTINUED —

Think of red velvet as devil's food that has been kicked up a notch. Like a lot of fancy-pants cakes, it's thought to be a Southern invention. Red on the inside, fluffy white frosting on the outside, it's "the Dolly Parton of cakes: a little bit tacky, but you love her," according to Atlanta food writer Angie Mosier. It was the signature dessert at New York's Waldorf-Astoria Hotel in the 1920s, but fell out of favor after WWII, when red food dye was believed to cause cancer. Thankfully, food chemists have gotten smarter, so red food dye is back in.

So is red velvet cake, thanks in part to that horrible 1989 film *Steel Magnolias* (starring Dolly Parton, interestingly enough). I HATED it. But there was a scene with an armadillo-shaped red velvet cake, frosted with gray icing. It was very tacky (like the movie) and blindingly red inside.

Jessica Simpson, a Texan, chose red velvet cake for her nonstick 2002 nuptials to Nick Lachey. On one level this is not surprising, because Jessica is a big Dolly Parton fan. Her cake, thankfully, was not shaped like an armadillo.

Red velvet cakes traditionally contain cocoa, though I have tasted some that didn't seem to. They were fine cakes, but not as good. Kind of like drag queens doing Dolly. Cocoa adds flavor and enhances the red color.

Quick question here: do you know why devil's food cake is called that? Some surmise that it's just so delicious that to eat it is a sin, but the late Supreme Master Extraordinaire of All Things Culinary and authoritative cookbook author James Beard thought it was named after its reddish tint. The tint is produced when cocoa is present in a recipe containing baking soda and an acid (such as buttermilk or vinegar), to which the baking soda reacts. According to one theory, prior to the 1920s, home bakers began adding beet juice or red food dye to exaggerate the redness of devil's food cake, and the result was red velvet cake.

I hate beets. I also hate red food dye because frequently red velvet recipes call for a whole bottle and if you're not careful, your kitchen will look like the crime scene from *Fargo*, with the KitchenAid mixer standing in for the wood chipper. And really, it doesn't take that much red food coloring to make a cake red. So I use half the recommended amount. Because I'm working with dark chocolate, my red velvet cake isn't blindingly red; it's more of a deep, chocolaty red, a shade down from burgundy.

The foundation cake for this recipe is from *Southern Living* magazine. I substituted sour cream for buttermilk. Originally, this cake called for unsweetened cocoa, but I love Hershey's Dutch process Special Dark Cocoa too much, so baking powder has been added.

After trying this recipe, if you want an easy, tasty, and very moist yellow cake perfect for frosting, simply skip the cocoa, baking powder, and, of course, the food coloring.

Dark-Chocolate Red Velvet Cake — CONTINUED

TO MAKE THE CAKE

1. Position a rack in lower third of the oven and preheat to 325 degrees F. Prepare the cake pans.
2. Cream the butter in a mixer on medium speed, then gradually add the sugars, beating well. Add the eggs, one at a time, beating well after each addition. Add the vanilla extract and beat until blended.
3. In a separate bowl, dry whisk the flour, baking soda, cocoa, and baking powder together.
4. Add 1 cup of the floured cocoa mixture and ⅓ cup of the sour cream alternately, beating well after each addition. Repeat until all the flour mixture and sour cream have been blended in.
5. Add the food coloring and beat well. Use a spatula to scrape down the sides of the bowl and stir up the batter at the bottom, then beat again.
6. Poor the batter into the prepared pans and place pans close to the center of the oven rack, but not touching. Bake for 45 minutes, or until the cake layers test done.
7. Cool the layers in the pans for 10 minutes, then unmold onto cake racks to cool to room temperature.

TO MAKE THE FROSTING

8. Cream the butter and cream cheese together at medium speed. Gradually add the confectioners' sugar, beating until light and fluffy. Add the vanilla extract and mix until just incorporated.
9. Assemble and frost the layers in the usual way, frosting the sides last, after the crown.

Triple Chocolate Orange Passion Cake

YOU'LL NEED

Two 8-inch or 9-inch round cake pans
A medium bowl
A microwave-safe bowl

FOR THE CAKE

2 large eggs
Two 1-ounce squares unsweetened chocolate
2 cups cake flour
2 cups sugar
½ cup Dutch process unsweetened cocoa
1 teaspoon baking powder
½ teaspoon salt
½ teaspoon milk
¼ cup vegetable oil
1 teaspoon vanilla extract
Grated zest and juice of 1 orange

FOR THE FROSTING

6 tablespoons unsalted butter, at room temperature
One 16-ounce box confectioners' sugar (about 3¾ cups)
½ cup heavy whipping cream
¼ teaspoon salt
¼ teaspoon orange oil or orange extract (see Tip)
Two 1-ounce squares unsweetened chocolate

FOR DECORATION (OPTIONAL)

2 ounces bittersweet chocolate for dipping citrus slices
About 6 clementine or orange slices

Tip: Orange oil can be tricky to find. Depending on where you live and what's available, you might have to special order it, bringing us into the WALLET WARNING zone. Orange oil gives the cake an extra kick, but orange extract works fine.

TO MAKE THE CAKE

1. Center a rack and preheat the oven to 400 degrees F. Prepare the pans.
2. Put the eggs, still in their shells, in a bowl filled with hot tap water.
3. Bring about 2 cups of water to boil. While the water's heating up . . .
4. In a microwave-safe bowl, melt the unsweetened chocolate squares in the microwave on high power.

CONTINUED —

So, a special occasion came to pass in the office: one of my coworkers, an avid cake eater, was leaving NPR to work for Marketplace. I asked Jeremy Hobson what he'd like for his final Monday cake, and he said, "Fried Pies." And I said, "EEEEEEEH! Wrong answer. Please play again." "How about chocolate orange cake?" he countered. We bickered back and forth over the phone (which was funny because we could see each other's faces since we sat in catty-corner cubicles) until he convinced me that chocolate and orange were a good flavor combination and worth four hours of my weekend.

I found this recipe in an interesting book called *Cakes from Scratch in Half the Time* by Linda West Eckhardt. Linda has reformulated classic cake recipes so that they mix in 20 percent less time and bake in 30 percent less time. The key is to bake them in thin aluminum pans at higher temperatures, the way professional bakers do. My wee oven is notoriously cranky, and at this point in my life I'm not about to get a whole new set of bakeware, but Linda's recipes still taste great.

Because of the cranky oven, they took the usual amount of time to bake, but I did save on some mixing time. I used those extra 10 minutes to watch silly cat videos on YouTube. The boxing cats just kill me.

Triple Chocolate **Orange Passion Cake** — CONTINUED

5. In the mixer bowl, dry whisk the flour, sugar, cocoa, baking powder, and salt together. Beat on low speed for 30 seconds, then, while beating continuously, add the milk, oil, eggs, vanilla extract, and orange zest, one at a time. Stop beating, scrape down the sides of the bowl, then beat for 2 minutes at medium speed.

6. In a heat-proof measuring cup, measure your orange juice and add enough of the boiling water to make 1 cup. Add the melted chocolate and stir together. Add this mixture to the batter. Stir the batter with a wooden spoon or spatula until just blended.

7. Divide the batter among the prepared pans and bake 15 to 20 minutes, until the cake layers test done.

This is where things did not go as planned because I was using thicker pans than recommended in that wee, cranky oven. If you're in the same situation, my best advice is to check the cakes after 15 minutes, then again in 5-minute intervals until the cake layers test done. The second time you make this cake, you'll have a better idea of how long it will take you. The layers needed 25 minutes in my oven.

8. Cool the cake layers in the pans for 5 minutes, then unmold onto cake racks and cool to room temperature.

TO MAKE THE FROSTING

9. Cream the butter in the mixer on medium speed, gradually adding half of the confectioners' sugar. Add the cream, the rest of the confectioners' sugar, the salt, and orange oil or orange extract.

10. In a microwave-safe bowl, melt the chocolate in the microwave on high power. Using a spatula, add the chocolate to the frosting and beat until smooth and fluffy. Let the frosting stand while the cake layers cool.

11. Construct the cake, frosting in the usual manner, the crown first, and then the sides.

TO DECORATE THE CAKE (OPTIONAL)

12. Melt 2 ounces bittersweet chocolate in a small microwave-safe bowl. Dip the tips of the clementine or orange slices into the chocolate, and set aside on wax paper to cool. Arrange the slices as a border on the cake plate or arrange on top of the cake.

German's Chocolate Cake

ACHTUNG! NICHT DEUTSCH!

YOU'LL NEED

Two 8-inch or 9-inch round cake pans
3 or 4 medium bowls
A whisk attachment and extra bowl for mixer
A food processor
A double boiler, real or improvised

FOR THE CAKE

One 4-ounce package Baker's German's Sweet Chocolate
½ cup boiling water
2 sticks (1 cup) unsalted butter, at room temperature
2 cups sugar
4 large eggs, separated
1 teaspoon vanilla extract
2 cups all-purpose flour
1 teaspoon baking soda
½ teaspoon salt
1 cup buttermilk

CONTINUED —

I don't know how these urban myths get started. You think a mouthful of Pop Rocks and a swig of Coca-Cola killed Mikey, the kid from the Life cereal commercials, and you think over in Germany they eat German chocolate cake. Well, Mikey didn't die from the Pop Rocks Coca-Cola combo, and in Germany they eat German chocolate cake only when idiot Americans pop over with what they think is a native dessert. The culprit here for international gastronomical misunderstanding is a possessive *s* gone AWOL.

This cake should really be called *German's* Chocolate Cake. And the inventor, Sam German, wasn't German; he was English. In 1852 he developed a brand of chocolate bar for Baker's Chocolate Company that tasted somewhat like milk chocolate. Flash forward 103 years, when an unnamed Dallas housewife sent this recipe to a Texas newspaper, as Texas housewives are wont to do (remember Tunnel of Fudge Cake, page 89). The Lone Star state loved it. The company that owned Baker's Chocolate, General Foods, thought "cah-CHING!" So, it sent out copies of the recipe to the nation's newspapers. German's Chocolate Cakes started popping up in kitchens across America, and Baker's sold a lot of German's chocolate. They still do. And that's why you're reading about German's Chocolate Cake today.

The cake itself has a soft, moist, bouncy, milk-chocolaty crumb. The filling and topping contain a sweet 'n' crunchy mix of coconut and pecans stirred into a sweet 'n' smooth spread. Korva Coleman in Newscast especially likes it, and she's not crazy about coconut. There's an optional chocolate frosting that should be applied to the sides only. The cake is fine with or without it. You can also double the recipe for the filling and topping and apply some to the sides.

This cake is also a good choice for dark chocolate lovers who are feeling a bit burnt out on dark chocolate, but are not ready to fully detox at the Promises L.A. rehab facility yet.

German's Chocolate Cake — CONTINUED

FOR THE FILLING AND TOPPING

1⅓ cups pecans
1¾ cups flaked coconut
One 14-ounce can sweetened condensed milk
½ cup water
3 large egg yolks
1 stick (½ cup) unsalted butter
1 teaspoon vanilla extract

Tip: If you're planning to only use the filling/topping and you want to cover the sides of the cake with it, double this recipe.

FOR THE CHOCOLATE FROSTING (OPTIONAL)

2 ounces Baker's German's Sweet Chocolate
1 stick (½ cup) unsalted butter, at room temperature
1½ cups confectioners' sugar
1 teaspoon vanilla extract
1½ tablespoons milk

TO MAKE THE CAKE

1. Center a rack and preheat the oven to 350 degrees F. Prepare the cake pans.
2. In a heat-proof bowl, break up the German's chocolate into small squares. Add the boiling water and stir until smooth.

If you're stirring, stirring, stirring, and the chocolate refuses to melt further, just microwave it in the bowl at high power for 1 minute, then stir again.

3. In a mixer on medium speed, cream the butter, then gradually add the sugar, beating well.
4. Add the yolks to the creamed mixture and beat thoroughly. Beat in the chocolate and vanilla extract.
5. In a separate bowl, dry whisk the flour, baking soda, and salt together.
6. Add half the flour to the batter and then half of the buttermilk, beating well after each addition. Repeat with the remaining flour and buttermilk, and beat to blend well.
7. Set the batter aside. Attach the whisk to the mixer and set up a clean, dry bowl.
8. With the mixer on high speed, beat the egg whites to the stiff peak stage.
9. Fold the egg whites into the batter. This will take about 15 full rotations of the bowl.
10. Pour the batter into the prepared pans and bake for 30 minutes, or until the layers test done.
11. Remove the layers from the oven and cool in the pans for 10 minutes. Unmold onto cake racks and let cool to room temperature before dividing, filling, and frosting.

TO MAKE THE FILLING AND TOPPING

Ever worked with sweetened condensed milk? Have a spatula handy: It's the consistency of caramel and as resistant to coming out of that can as a mad kitty in a carrier at the vet's. A spatula is neither helpful nor recommended in that particular instance, but essential in this one.

12. Set aside 6 nice-looking pecan halves for garnish. Then, in a food processor, pulse the remaining pecans and the coconut together until the mix is moderately chopped.

(ACHTUNG! If you're planning to use the chocolate frosting, this is a good time to jump ahead and melt your chocolate for it. By the time you're done with the filling, the chocolate will be cool enough to use in the frosting.)

13. Stir together the condensed milk, water, and egg yolks over simmering water in a double boiler and continue stirring until the mixture has thickened. Then add the butter and vanilla extract and whisk until smooth. Remove from the heat and add the chopped pecans and coconut. Set aside.

FOR THE CHOCOLATE FROSTING (OPTIONAL)

14. Melt the chocolate in the top of a double boiler over simmering water, or microwave at high power for 1 minute in a microwave-safe bowl. Set aside and let cool.
15. In the bowl of a mixer on medium speed, beat the butter with the cooled chocolate. Gradually beat in the confectioners' sugar. Beat in the vanilla extract and then gradually add the milk, beating until the frosting has a spreadable consistency.

TO CONSTRUCT THE CAKE

16. Divide and separate your layers.
17. Place the bottom layer on a serving plate and spread the filling over the top. Repeat with the remaining layers, until you've reached the crown. Spread the filling evenly over the top and garnish with the reserved 6 pecan halves if desired.
18. If using the chocolate frosting, frost only the sides of the cake. If you own a pastry bag with nozzles and are feeling extra sassy, pipe a frosting design along top and bottom edges of the cake.

19. Stand back and admire your handiwork. Take a picture. Practice a coy faux-humble look in the mirror before serving, in preparation for the laying on of compliments upon your noble brow.

Angel Food Cake NOT AS HARD OR AS CALORIC AS YOU THINK

YOU'LL NEED

A 10-inch tube pan
A whisk attachment for mixer
A long-necked glass bottle, such as a beer, wine, or salad-dressing bottle (do not use plastic)

1 cup sifted cake flour
1¼ cups sugar
1 cup egg whites (8 to 10 large egg whites)
1 teaspoon cream of tartar
½ teaspoon salt
1 teaspoon vanilla extract
¼ teaspoon almond extract

1. Center a rack and preheat the oven to 375 degrees F. Line the tube pan with parchment paper, but DO NOT SPRAY or GREASE the pan.
2. Dry whisk the flour and only ¼ cup of the sugar together. Set aside.
3. With the mixer on medium-high and the whisk attachment in place, whisk the egg whites, cream of tartar, and salt until the mixture is frothy.
4. Add the remaining cup of sugar gradually, whisking furiously (Vigorously! Fiercely!) after each addition. Think about all those Pennsylvania children who need spanking and can't get a good one these days because their mamas' arms have atrophied as a result of their reliance on electric mixers.
5. Increase the mixer speed to high and continue beating until the egg whites are at the stiff peak stage, but are not dry.
6. Shift down to medium speed, add the flavorings, and beat until just incorporated. DO NOT OVERBEAT.
7. Remove the bowl from the mixer. Sprinkle ¼ cup of your flour mixture over your egg whites and fold into the egg whites. This may take as many as 15 to 20 full rotations of the bowl.
8. Continue folding the flour into the batter, ¼ cup at a time, until all the flour is completely incorporated into the egg whites.
9. Pour the batter into the parchment paper–lined, UNGREASED tube pan. Avoid trapping big air bubbles as best you can: use the spatula to release any big pockets of trapped air and to smooth the top of the batter.
10. Center the pan on the oven rack and bake for 35 to 40 minutes, until the cake tests done.
11. Cool the cake in the pan for 5 minutes. Then, invert the pan and slip the tube portion over the neck of a long-necked bottle, so the cake is hanging upside down. We do this because Angel Food Cake is delicate and while cooling, it can actually collapse on itself if left upright. Don't worry—it's not going to fall out of the pan while it's upside down, either. We didn't grease that pan, remember?

12. When the cake is fully cooled, turn the pan right side up. Take a rubber spatula or dull butter knife (I remove the rubber from my spatula and just use the wooden handle) and carefully insert it between the pan and the cake, pushing very slightly against the spongy cake. Do this gently all the way around the sides of the pan and around the center tube. Then invert the pan onto a plate or cake rack. The cake should release itself from the pan. If not, try loosening the cake again by pushing against the sides of the cake with a spatula or knife, then unmold.

By now, you're an experienced hand with separating eggs and whipping up egg whites, so making that light, spongy, cloudlike cake known as Angel Food will be No Big Whoop.

This is the main thing I want to emphasize: If you haven't been using the triple-bowl method for separating your egg whites, for Pete's sake, use it now. To review: This is the method where you

1. Break your egg over a clean bowl, allowing only the egg white to slip into said clean bowl while hanging onto your yolk, then

2. Deposit your yolk into a separate bowl specifically for egg yolks before

3. Pouring your egg white into a collecting bowl specifically for egg whites.

The reason (and I know I've said this before, but it bears repeating): With 8 to 10 eggs to separate for this recipe, you do not, I repeat DO NOT want to break egg number 8, 9, or 10 over your carefully collected egg whites and have that one errant runny yolk ruin the entire batch of whites. When broken yolk infiltrates egg whites, they will not form stiff peaks. You will not have an Angel Food Cake. You will have failed. There is no crying in baseball, and there is no crying over ruined egg whites, especially when you knew better.

Tough love—that's what Angel Food Cake is all about, Toots.

OK, not really. Tough arms, maybe, but not tough love. I'm thinking about the late nineteenth century, when Angel Food Cake started showing up in American cookbooks. There were no electric mixers, just Pennsylvania Dutch women eatin' their spinach and whisking and folding the heck out of their egg whites.

Can you imagine getting a spanking from one of those gals? OW-wee OW OW! Now, it's only believed that this cake originated with the Pennsylvania Dutch. In his book *American Food: The Gastronomic Story*, Evan Jones surmises that this cake was developed because those thrifty Quaker State women had just finished making noodles, which require egg yolks, and couldn't stand to waste all those egg whites. Some call it thrifty; I call it Spank-Your-Pennsylvania-Dutch-Grandma delicious!

Unlike most cakes, Angel Food Cake is best cut with a serrated knife, the kind you'd normally use for bread. It also doesn't make neat thin slices, and because it's so light and spongy, people tend to want chunks rather than slices anyway. So plan to serve between 16 and 20 people.

This is another gem from that 1969 Culinary Arts Institute pamphlet.

Chocolate Angel Food Cake

FOR THAT SAINT WITH PMS

This has much of the same technique as the previous recipe, but the ingredients have slightly different proportions and cocoa has been added. Your Angel Food aficionados will think it's just OK, but the chocolate hounds will love it.

Just like regular Angel Food Cake, you'll need to cut this with a serrated bread knife and serve it in chunks rather than slices. Be prepared to serve 16 to 20 people.

This is also from that 1969 Culinary Arts Institute pamplet. A gift that keeps on giving.

YOU'LL NEED

A 10-inch tube pan
A whisk attachment for mixer
A glass beer, wine, or salad dressing bottle

¾ cup sifted cake flour
¼ cup unsweetened cocoa (NOT Dutch process)
1¼ cups egg whites (10 to 12 large eggs)
½ teaspoon salt
1 teaspoon cream tartar
1¼ cups sugar
1 teaspoon vanilla extract

1. Center a rack and preheat the oven to 375 degrees F. Do not spray or grease the pan; just line it with parchment paper.
2. Dry whisk the flour and cocoa together.
3. With the mixer on medium-high speed and the whisk attachment in place, beat the egg whites and salt together until the egg whites are foamy. Add the cream of tartar, increase the mixer speed to high, and continue beating until stiff peaks form.
4. Remove the bowl from the mixer. Fold in the sugar, ¼ cup at a time, until all the sugar is fully incorporated. This will take up to 15 full rotations of the bowl.
5. Fold in the vanilla extract. This will take about 1 rotation of the bowl.
6. Sprinkle ¼ cup of the flour and cocoa mixture over the egg whites and fold until incorporated, about 15 to 20 full rotations of the bowl. Repeat 3 more times until all of the dry mixture is fully incorporated.
7. Pour the batter into the ungreased tube pan. Use a spatula to release any big air bubbles and to smooth over the top of the batter.
8. Center on the oven rack and bake 35 to 45 minutes, or until the cake tests done.
9. Cool the cake in the pan for 5 minutes, then invert onto the glass bottle to finish cooling.
10. Turn the pan right side up and insert a rubber spatula or dull butter knife between pan and the sides of the cake. Gently push the cake away from the sides of the pan and the center tube. Invert the pan onto a plate or cake rack. The cake should slide out of the pan. If not, try loosening the cake again by pushing against the sides of the cake with a spatula or knife, then unmold.

Lady and Lord Baltimore Cakes

A DEMI-ROYAL EXPERIENCE WITH DIVINITY FROSTING

"I should like a slice, if you please, of Lady Baltimore," I said with extreme formality. I returned to the table and she brought me the cake, and I had my first felicitous meeting with Lady Baltimore. Oh, my goodness! Did you ever taste it? It's all soft, and it's in layers, and it has nuts—but I can't write any more about it; my mouth waters too much. Delighted surprise caused me once more to speak aloud, and with my mouth full, "But, dear me, this is delicious."

—from Owen Wister's 1906 novel *Lady Baltimore*

CONTINUED —

Considering the frightfully, yet delightfully, figgity-stickity state of a Lady Baltimore cake, I seriously expect Owen Wister's narrator to have actually said aloud, with his mouth full, "Boof, duere moof, wiff iff dulufoff!"

And is it me, or is there something implicitly naughty about that passage? *Lady Baltimore* is a romance novel set in Charleston, South Carolina. The central character was based on a real-life Charleston belle, Alicia Rhett Mayberry.[1] In the novel, Lady Baltimore named her cake after herself.[2] Naturally, the reading public wanted the recipe, which was actually a *fig*ment of Wister's mind. Or a Fig Newton of Wister's mind, because actually, this recipe does kind of taste like a Fig Newton crossed with a Twinkie.

ANYWAY, Wister's cake may have been based on another cake, a variation of the Queen Cake popular at that time. *Supposedly*, the cake that came to be known as Lady Baltimore Cake was developed at the end of the nineteenth century at a Charleston tea room named the Lady Baltimore.[3] *Supposedly* they baked and shipped one of these cakes to Master Wister every Christmas. *Apparently* the first mention of an actual recipe appeared in a number of newspapers in 1906, the year *Lady Baltimore* was published.

There are a number of different Lady Baltimore recipes out there, but they're all basically the same: a white cake with layers of chopped-up raisins, figs, and nuts mixed with a fluffy, marshmallow-like frosting.

My recipe comes from that 1969 pamphlet published by the Culinary Arts Institute. There's no romance in this pamphlet, just 200 cakes, including one for Lord Baltimore. Given that m'Lady is made with egg whites, it seems m'Lord was developed for the leftover egg yolks. Also, in the manly version, the cake is yellow and buttery, and the filling includes macaroon crumbs, pecans, orange extract, blanched almonds, and candied cherries (Lord Baltimore must have been hypoglycemic!). Both cakes are frosted with divinity frosting, which requires a candy thermometer and NO distractions!

1. Quick! Where were Rhett Butler's relatives from in *Gone with the Wind*? Yes! Charleston! Literary coincidence? I think not.
2. I would have named my cake Henrietta Billingsworth, but then again I'm not the subject of an innuendo-filled romance novel. Yet.
3. Thank God it wasn't named the Queen's Head and Artichoke—that would have been a HORRIBLE name for a cake. Or a novel. Maybe not for a memoir.

Lady and Lord Baltimore **Cakes** — CONTINUED

Lady Baltimore

YOU'LL NEED

Two 8-inch or two 9-inch round cake pans
A whisk attachment and extra bowl for mixer
A medium bowl
2 rubber spatulas
A food processor

FOR THE CAKE

2 sticks (1 cup) unsalted butter, at room temperature
2 cups sugar
3½ cups sifted cake flour
4 teaspoons baking powder
½ teaspoon salt
1 cup milk
1 teaspoon vanilla extract
1 cup egg whites (8 to 10 large egg whites)

FOR THE LADY'S FILLING

2 cups raisins
2 cups figs
3 cups nuts (I recommend a mix of pecans and almonds)
1 teaspoon lemon extract

Divinity Frosting (page 190)

TO MAKE THE LADY'S CAKE

1. Center a rack and preheat the oven to 375 degrees F. Prepare the pans.
2. With the mixer on medium speed, cream the butter. Gradually add the sugar, beating until smooth.
3. In a separate bowl, dry whisk the flour, baking powder, and salt together.
4. Add 1 cup of the flour mixture and ⅓ cup of milk alternately, beating well after each addition. Repeat until all of the flour mixture and milk are blended in.
5. Add the vanilla extract and beat well. The batter will be thicker than you're used to. If it's way too thick, add 1 extra tablespoon of milk and beat. Set aside.
6. Remove the paddle or the beaters, attach the whisk, and set a clean, dry mixing bowl in place. Whip the egg whites on high speed until you reach the stiff peak stage.
7. Remove the bowl from the mixer. Fold half the egg whites into the batter until completely incorporated, then fold in the remaining egg whites.
8. Pour the batter into the prepared cake pans and bake for 25 minutes, or until the layers test done. Cool the layers in the pans 10 minutes. Unmold onto cake racks and cool to room temperature.

TO MAKE THE LADY'S FILLING

9. If you wish, set aside a few pecan halves to decorate the top of the cake.
10. In your food processor, chop the raisins, figs, and remaining nuts with the lemon extract until medium-coarse in texture. Set aside.

CONTINUED —

Skip ahead to page 190 for Divinity Frosting directions if you're making just the Lady Baltimore Cake. Then, for directions on assembling the cake, see page 191.

Lord Baltimore

YOU'LL NEED

Two 8-inch or two 9-inch round cake pans
A whisk attachment and extra bowl for mixer
2 or 3 medium bowls
2 rubber spatulas
A food processor

FOR THE CAKE

2/3 cup egg yolks (7 or 8 large egg yolks)
1½ sticks (3/4 cup) unsalted butter, at room temperature
1¼ cups sugar
½ teaspoon lemon extract
1 teaspoon vanilla extract
2½ cups sifted cake flour
3 teaspoons baking powder
½ teaspoon salt
3/4 cup milk

FOR THE MANLY FILLING

1 cup dry macaroon crumbs
½ cup pecans
½ cup almonds, chopped
24 candied cherries, quartered
½ teaspoon orange extract
4 teaspoons lemon juice

Divinity Frosting (page 190)

TO MAKE *ES MUY MACHO* CAKE

1. Center a rack and preheat the oven to 375 degrees F. Prepare the pans.
2. With the mixer on medium speed, beat the egg yolks until thick and light yellow. Set aside. Clean the paddle attachment or beaters and set a clean mixing bowl in place.
3. Cream the butter on medium speed, gradually adding the sugar and beating well. Add the lemon extract and vanilla extract and beat the mixture until it is extremely creamy. Super creamy.
4. Add the egg yolks to the creamed mixture and beat for 5 minutes on medium speed.
5. In a separate bowl, dry whisk the flour, baking powder, and salt together.
6. Add a third of the flour mixture to the creamed mixture, followed by a third of the milk, and beat well. Repeat two more times to use up all of the flour and milk. Beat for 2 more minutes at medium-high speed.
7. Pour the batter into the prepared pans and bake 20 to 25 minutes, or until the cake layers test done.
8. Cool the layers in the pans for 10 minutes. Unmold onto cake racks and cool to room temperature.

TO MAKE THE FILLING

9. If you wish, set aside a few pecan halves or whole cherries to decorate the top of the cake before making the filling.
10. In your food processor, chop the macaroons, pecans, almonds, and candied cherries with the orange extract and lemon juice until medium-coarse. Set aside while you make the Divinity Frosting.

CONTINUED –

Lady and Lord Baltimore **Cakes** – CONTINUED

And now, the moment we've all been waiting for . . . DIVINITY FROSTING!

Seriously, have NO distractions when you're making this. Take no phone calls. Answer no e-mails. Text no friends. Shoo your children out of the kitchen or, heck, out of the house. Lock up your pets. Tell your spouse or partner to GO AWAY AND NOT COME BACK UNTIL YOU SAY SO. Also, if you have an apron, wear it. This part can get messy.

You're going to be dealing with hot (as in 268 degrees F) sugar syrup. It is CRITICAL that you have a candy thermometer. One with a clip is ideal: you can clip it to the side of the pan. Do not proceed further until you go out and get one. Seriously. This has to be done precisely, or it won't work at all.

This recipe is enough for both the frosting and filling of one cake. Double the quantity of the frosting if you're making both the Lord and Lady Baltimore Cakes at one time.

Divinity Frosting

YOU'LL NEED

A whisk attachment for the mixer
A heavy saucepan
A candy thermometer
Oven mitts

4 large egg whites
3 cups sugar
¾ cup water
¼ teaspoon cream of tartar
2 teaspoons vanilla extract

11. With the mixer on high speed and the whisk attachment in place, beat the egg whites until they have stiff peaks. Stop the mixer.
12. Combine the sugar, water, and cream of tartar in a heavy saucepan. Insert your candy thermometer. Turn your burner as high as it will go, then STAND THERE AND WATCH the temperature rise on the thermometer. Do not stir yourself or the pot. STAND THERE AND WATCH.
13. When the sugar syrup reaches 230 degrees F, turn your mixer to medium-high speed. Put on your oven mitts. In less than a minute, the syrup will reach 238 degrees F. When it does, remove the saucepan from the heat and, holding the candy thermometer steady in one mitted hand, pour a THIRD of the hot syrup down the inside of the mixing bowl. DO NOT POUR ONTO THE WHISK. Aim for the side of the bowl. Return the saucepan to the heat. Leave the mixer mixing.
14. When the syrup reaches 248 degrees F, remove the saucepan from the heat and, using the same technique, pour HALF the remaining hot syrup into the mixing bowl. Return the saucepan to the heat. Leave the mixer mixing.
15. When the syrup reaches 268 degrees F, turn off the heat and pour the remaining syrup into the mixing bowl, still aiming at the sides of the bowl.
16. Add the vanilla extract and beat until the mixture is thick enough to spread. It will be sticky. It will be gooey. It will be rather warm. When it cools off and is ready to use, it will taste divine.

TO CONSTRUCT THE CAKES

17. Spoon (or spackle, 'cause I'm not kidding about the goo) half of your frosting into a separate bowl. Stir in the filling.

18. Divide and separate your layers as desired (see page 159 if you need a refresher course). Arrange wax paper strips on the serving plate so the edges of the bottom layer will sit on the strips, and transfer the bottom layer to the plate.

19. Put a heaping dollop of your filling onto the center of the layer. CAREFULLY spread it toward the edges, moving your spatula in ONE direction. This stuff is unlike any frosting you've ever worked with before, and if you try to add more frosting to the center of the top and then spread back and forth, you're going to tear up the tender cake crumb beneath it. When you have to add more filling, literally spackle it on where needed and continue to carefully spread in one direction.

20. Add the remaining layers, one at a time, spreading each one with filling, until you reach the top or crowning layer.

21. Using a clean spatula, begin applying the frosting to the crown, starting with a heaping dollop in the middle. Again, move the frosting in one direction and spackle additional frosting where needed.

22. Get a butter knife and remove crumbs and spillover filling from the sides before frosting. Then go at it, again making sure to move in one direction.

23. Garnish the cake if you're feeling special: Use the pecan halves or candied cherries you've saved and arrange on the crown of the cake. Be creative. Make a spiral, a figure 8, your boss's initials, whatever. Let the cake sit for 15 to 20 minutes, then remove the wax strips.

"Miss Maudie baked a Lane Cake so loaded with shinny it made me tight."

—Scout Finch, in *To Kill a Mockingbird*

Lane Cake

YOU'LL NEED

Two 8-inch or 9-inch round cake pans
A whisk attachment and extra bowl for mixer
A medium bowl
A food processor
A double boiler, real or improvised

FOR THE CAKE

2 sticks (1 cup) unsalted butter, at room temperature
2 cups sugar
1 teaspoon vanilla extract
3¼ cups cake flour
3½ teaspoons baking powder
¼ teaspoon salt
1 cup milk
1 cup egg whites (8 to 10 large egg whites)

FOR THE FILLING AND FROSTING

2½ cups pecans
2 cups unsweetened shredded coconut
2 cups raisins
1 cup candied cherries, quartered
1 teaspoon ground mace
½ teaspoon salt
8 large egg yolks
1¼ cups sugar
3 tablespoons grated orange zest
1 teaspoon orange extract
⅓ cup bourbon (apple cider or grape or cherry juice may be substituted)

CONTINUED —

When I first read Harper Lee's *To Kill a Mockingbird* in seventh grade, I identified with Scout Finch. She's the young daughter of Atticus Finch, the attorney assigned to defend a black man accused of raping a white woman in a small, Southern town during the late 1930s. But as I've gotten older, I see myself in other characters, particularly Miss Maudie Atkinson, the middle-aged widow with the tart tongue.

Miss Maudie is a female role model for the motherless Scout. In a world dominated by men, she does as she pleases, wearing men's overalls while gardening, but transforming into a "lady" every day after her five o'clock bath. Though she's a lady, Miss Maudie does not suffer fools.

When she's angry, she's very angry. When she's friendly, she bakes. In fact, we're told early in the book that Miss Maudie bakes the best cakes in the neighborhood.

One of her specialties is a Lane Cake. She bakes one for Mr. Avery when he helps save her furniture from a house fire, and she bakes one for Aunty Alexandra when she moves to Maycomb to look after Scout and her brother Jem.

I've always wondered what was in a Lane Cake, other than sugar and enough shinny that one slice can make a grade-schooler tight. So I looked it up. A lane cake is a white or yellow cake layered with a combination of chopped nuts, dried fruit, coconut soused in apple cider (for the foot-washing Baptists and the Mormons) or shinny such as bourbon (for dirty-footed Baptists, the Jack Mormons, and the rest of us). It's believed to have originated in Clayton, Alabama, with one Emma Rylander Lane. She won a prize for it at the state fair. The recipe was first printed in 1898, but it has been modified many times since.

This recipe is adapted from Diana's Desserts, a Web site for home bakers run by Diana Baker Woodall, who lives in Sonoma County, California. It's definitely worth checking out.

Since I'm not a foot-washing Baptist or a Mormon, my Lane Cake is full of shinny. It doesn't make my co-workers tight, but my boss, Christopher Turpin, was overheard saying, with his mouth full, "OH MY GOD! You can REALLY taste the bourbon in this one!" Chris really likes booze in his cakes.

This is a cake that needs to mature for 1 or 2 days, by the way. Lets the crumb absorb more of the hooch.

Lane Cake — CONTINUED

TO MAKE THE CAKE

1. Center a rack and preheat the oven to 375 degrees F. Prepare the pans.
2. With a mixer on medium speed, cream the butter, then gradually add the sugar and beat until light and fluffy. Add the vanilla extract and beat until incorporated.
3. In a separate bowl, dry whisk the flour, baking powder, and salt together.
4. Add about 1 cup of the flour mixture and ⅓ cup of the milk alternately, beating well after each addition. Repeat until all of the flour mixture and milk are blended into the batter. It will be thick, almost doughy.
5. Set aside the batter. With the whisk attachment, beat the egg whites in a clean, dry bowl on high speed until stiff, but not dry.
6. Fold a fourth of the egg whites into the batter. This will take about 10 full rotations of the bowl. Fold in the remaining egg whites until fully incorporated, about 20 full rotations of the bowl.
7. Pour the batter into the prepared cake pans and bake for 20 to 25 minutes, until the cake layers test done.
8. Cool the layers in the pans for 10 minutes, then unmold onto cake racks to finish cooling.

TO MAKE THE FILLING AND FROSTING

9. Set aside 6 nice-looking pecan halves. Put the remaining pecans into the food processor and pulse to coarsely chop. Remove and set aside.
10. Put the coconut and raisins in the food processor and pulse to coarsely chop. Transfer to a medium bowl.
11. Add the quartered cherries to the chopped coconut and raisins. Then add all but ½ cup of the chopped pecans. Stir in the mace and salt. Set aside.

12. In the top of a double boiler over simmering water, stir together the egg yolks, sugar, orange zest, and orange extract until the sugar is dissolved and the mixture is thick enough to coat the back of a wooden spoon. Do not allow the water in the bottom of the double boiler to boil, or the eggs might scramble.
13. Remove from the heat and stir in the dried fruit and nut mixture. Stir in the bourbon. Allow to cool thoroughly before filling and frosting the cake.

TO CONSTRUCT THE CAKE

14. When the cake layers and filling are completely cooled, divide and separate the cake layers as you please. Spread filling on each layer before you position another on top. Spread filling on the crown. If you like, spread the filling on the sides, too.
15. Sprinkle 1/4 cup of the reserved chopped pecans on top of the cake. For an added touch, you can press the remaining 1/4 cup of chopped pecans onto the sides of the cake with your spatula.
16. Take the 6 nice-looking pecan halves you saved and press them into the top of the cake in a pleasing pattern.
17. Cover the cake loosely and allow to mature for at least a day before serving.

Appalachian Stack Cake

YOU'LL NEVER MAKE FUN OF MEEMAW AND PAWPAW AGAIN

YOU'LL NEED

A large saucepan
3 medium bowls
Two 8-inch round cake pans
5 plates

FOR THE FILLING

1⅛ pounds (about 3 cups) dried sliced apples
6 cups water
1 cup brown sugar (light or dark)
1 teaspoon ground ginger
1 teaspoon ground cinnamon
½ teaspoon ground allspice
½ teaspoon ground nutmeg

FOR THE COOKIE LAYERS

⅓ cup shortening
½ cup plus 2½ teaspoons sugar
1 large egg
4 cups all-purpose flour
1 teaspoon baking powder
1 teaspoon baking soda
½ teaspoon salt
½ cup molasses
½ cup buttermilk

CONTINUED —

And really, you shouldn't. Sometimes Meemaw and Pawpaw (whom you non-Southern types would call Grandmother and Grandfather) have a good thing going. Appalachian Stack Cake, a.k.a. dried apple stack cake, or Confederate old-fashioned stack cake, or Kentucky pioneer wash day cake, is one of them.

This is not a traditional layer cake by any means: there's no cake crumb to divide and layer. Instead, it's several giant molasses cookies pressed out flat and sprinkled with sugar. In between these cookies is a thick spread of spiced apple filling. This cake is the opposite of elegant; it looks like Lady Baltimore's poor mountain cousin, whom she doesn't admit to, but wow, how that cousin charms! What taste! She's like a Fig Newton too, but with apples! An Apple Newton!

Want a different kind of wedding cake? This might be the cake for you. According to mountain tradition, before a wedding, neighboring home bakers would each make a layer for the stack wedding cake. The number of layers in the cake were said to be a measure of the bride's popularity. Her family would prepare the apple filling themselves.

Just want to make your house smell good? This still might be the cake for you. It takes 45 minutes to 1 hour to make the apple filling, which includes brown sugar, ginger, cinnamon, allspice, and nutmeg. Burning a spice candle doesn't do half the job of this simmering mixture.

This is a recipe from *Southern Living* magazine's 2005 annual collection, which comes with this caveat: "Don't be tempted to eat the cake until it has stood for two days. This seasoning allows the moisture from the filling to soften the cake layers. This cake also freezes well."

Appalachian stack cake can be thinly sliced, but it's tricky. Plus people always come back for seconds, so count on serving 16 to 20.

Appalachian **Stack Cake** — CONTINUED

TO MAKE THE FILLING

(Yes, start the filling first!)

1. In a large saucepan over high heat, combine the apples and water. Bring to a boil, then reduce the heat, and simmer for 30 minutes.
2. Mix together the brown sugar and spices in a separate bowl, and set aside. While the apples are simmering, you can skip ahead to step 4 and begin the cookie layers.
3. After the apples have simmered for 30 minutes, stir the brown sugar and spices into the apple mixture, and return to a boil. Then reduce the heat and simmer for 15 to 30 minutes more, stirring occasionally, until most of the liquid has evaporated from the filling.

TO MAKE THE COOKIE LAYERS

4. Center a rack and preheat the oven to 400 degrees F. Prepare the cake pans.
5. With the mixer on medium speed, beat the shortening until creamed. Gradually add 1/2 cup of the sugar and beat until smooth. Add the egg and beat until the yellow disappears, about 5 minutes.
6. In a separate bowl, dry whisk the flour, baking powder, baking soda, and salt together.
7. In another bowl, stir the molasses and buttermilk together.
8. With the mixer on medium speed, gradually add 1 cup of flour mixture to the shortening mixture, then add 1/4 cup of the molasses mixture and beat well. Repeat until you've mixed in all of the flour mixture and molasses mixture. The batter will be doughy, and is likely to ball up once fully mixed.
9. Remove the dough from the mixing bowl and divide into 5 even portions.
10. Using your hands, pat 1 portion into a ball, then flatten into a fat disc. Place the disc in the center of the prepared baking pan. Press your fingers firmly on the center of the dough and begin spreading it out. Continue pressing, gradually spreading out the dough to the edge of the pan. Using 1 or 2 fingers, press any very ragged edges of the dough together to smooth out gaps. Use a fork to prick the dough several times. Sprinkle the dough evenly with 1/2 teaspoon of the remaining sugar.

11. Bake one pan at a time for 10 minutes. The cookie will look dry and will have pulled slightly away from the sides of the pan. Prepare the second pan while waiting for the first to be done.
12. Swap pans when the first cookie layer is done. Allow to cool for 5 minutes in the pan, then unmold the layer onto a baking rack to cool.

13. Spray the warm pan with baking spray and repeat step 10, spreading out the dough, pricking it with a fork, and sprinkling with sugar.
14. Finish baking the layers, and be sure to stir the apple filling occasionally. When the layers are done and the liquid has evaporated from the filling, allow everything to cool completely before constructing the cake.

TO CONSTRUCT THE CAKE

15. Set aside your best-looking layer for the top. Place your bottom layer on a serving plate, sugar side up. Spoon about a fifth of the apple filling onto the layer. Using a wooden spoon, spread out the filling almost to the edge of the layer. Add the next cookie layer, gently pressing down on the lower layer before adding filling. Repeat until you've crowned the cake with your top layer.
16. On the top of the cake, spoon the filling into the center and mound it instead of spreading it out all the way. You should have about 1½ to 2 inches of bare dough visible around the perimeter of the top layer.
17. Loosely cover the cake and let stand for 2 days at room temperature before serving.

Graham Cracker Cake

YOU'LL NEED

Two 8-inch or 9-inch round cake pans
A food processor
A whisk attachment and extra bowl for mixer
A pastry bag with a no. 5 plain nozzle
A large metal spatula
A small wire strainer

FOR THE CAKE

25 graham crackers, crumbled (about 3⅓ cups)
½ cup unsweetened shredded coconut
2½ teaspoons baking powder
1 stick (½ cup) unsalted butter, at room temperature
1 cup sugar
4 eggs, separated
1 teaspoon vanilla extract
1 cup milk
⅛ teaspoon cream of tartar

FOR THE MOCHA WHIPPED CREAM FILLING AND FROSTING

1¼ cups heavy whipping cream, well chilled
⅙ cup confectioners' sugar
1½ tablespoons unsweetened cocoa
½ teaspoon coffee (from your morning brew)
1 tablespoon Kalúha

FOR THE GARNISH

¼ teaspoon unsweetened cocoa
About ¼ cup raspberries (optional)

TO MAKE THE CAKE

1. Position a rack in the lower third of the oven and preheat to 350 degrees F. Prepare the cake pans.
2. In the food processor, pulse the graham cracker crumbs and coconut until very fine. Add the baking powder and pulse 6 to 8 times. Transfer to a bowl and set aside.
3. With the mixer on medium-high speed, cream the butter until smooth. Add the sugar gradually, beating until well blended. Scrape down the sides of the bowl occasionally.
4. Add the egg yolks, two at a time, beating for 1 minute after each addition. Scrape down the sides of the bowl. Beat for 1 extra minute. Blend in the vanilla extract.
5. Reduce the mixer speed to low. Add 1 cup of the crumb mixture along with ⅓ cup of milk and mix to blend in. Repeat until all the crumb mixture and milk are blended in. Scrape down the sides of the bowl and mix for 10 more seconds. Set the batter aside.

CONTINUED –

There was a time when I thought I could never get enough chocolate, but after making about a dozen different chocolate cakes, I've revised that notion. I'm now more interested in making cakes that are *augmented* by chocolate, rather than cakes that are simply a delivery vehicle for it. Here's one from *Great Cakes*, by Carole Walter, that fits the augmentation category.

It can be one pretty little cake, if you're willing to take the time. I did, and I wasn't sorry. All it required was a pastry bag with a medium-sized nozzle and 6 raspberries. But you can also apply the frosting with a spatula, as shown in our lovely photo. And for a tasty cake, make sure to buy good-quality graham crackers. If you want to divide the layers, double the frosting.

Graham Cracker Cake —CONTINUED

6. Set up the mixer with a clean, dry mixing bowl and whisk attachment. Beat the egg whites on medium speed until frothy. Add the cream of tartar and kick the mixer up to medium-high. Beat until the egg whites reach the firm peak stage. Do not overbeat.

7. Fold a quarter of the egg whites into the batter, taking about 5 full rotations of the bowl. Fold in the remaining egg whites, about 10 full turns.

8. Spoon the batter into the prepared pans, and smooth the surface with a spatula or wooden spoon.

9. Center the pans near the middle of the rack and bake for 25 or 30 minutes, or until the cake layers begin to come away from the sides of the pan and are springy to the touch.

10. Let the cakes cool in the pans for 10 minutes, then unmold onto the cake rack to cool completely.

TO MAKE THE FILLING AND FROSTING

11. Wash and dry your mixing bowl and whisk. Chill them in the freezer for 5 minutes.

12. Pour the cream into the chilled bowl and whip on medium-high speed for 1 or 2 minutes. Stir in the confectioners' sugar and cocoa, lower the speed to medium speed, and beat until the cream begins to thicken.

13. Add the coffee and Kalúha. Continue whipping until the cream reaches the soft peak stage, then remove from the mixer. Whisk by hand until the cream is thick. Refrigerate until you're ready to use.

TO CONSTRUCT THE CAKE

14. Fit a pastry bag with a no. 5 plain tube nozzle and fill the bag one-third full with the mocha whipped cream. Place the bottom cake layer on the serving plate.

15. Starting ½ inch from the edge of the cake, pipe a circle of cream around the layer. Fill the center with more cream, smoothing the surface with a large metal spatula.

16. Empty the remaining cream into the pastry bag. On the crown layer, pipe ½-inch dots, beginning at the outer edge. Each dot should touch the preceding one, forming a ring. Continue working toward the center of the cake until the entire surface is covered.

Note: You can also apply frosting with a spatula and skip the fancy pastry bag stuff.

17. Put the ¼ teaspoon of unsweetened cocoa in a fine-mesh strainer, and gently tap it to sprinkle the cocoa across the top of the cake. Add raspberries, if desired, in a decorative pattern. Refrigerate for at least 1 hour, and leave in the refrigerator until ready to serve.

Dark Chocolate Peppermint Pattie Cake

YOU'LL NEED

2 small saucepans
A food processor
A bottle (with lid) for the syrup
A fine-mesh strainer
A heavy saucepan
A medium strainer
A 9-inch springform pan
A double boiler, real or improvised
A whisk attachment and extra bowl for mixer
A bottle or jar (with lid) for the fudge sauce

FOR THE MINT SYRUP

2 cups packed fresh mint leaves
1¼ cups sugar
¾ cup water

FOR THE GANACHE

8 ounces semisweet or bittersweet chocolate
1 cup heavy whipping cream

CONTINUED →

Michele Norris told me about this strange humming sound she kept hearing the day I brought this cake in. There she was, typing away at her computer, writing an introduction to an interview she'd done with *Doonesbury* cartoonist Gary Trudeau, and she hears a series of "mmm-mmmm's" passing by her door. She heard actual language after the "mmmmmmm's", along the lines of "MmmmmmmGreg! You have got to try some of this cake!" "Mmm-mmmdid Susan get a slice of this cake?" "Mmmmmmmthis is the best cake Melissa's ever done!"

Well, the "mmmmmm's" have it. Dark Chocolate Peppermint Pattie Cake is rich, thick (like a torte), very chocolaty, and best when offset by whipped cream or vanilla ice cream.

This recipe comes from James Beard Award–winning pastry chef Karen Barker, the author of *Sweet Stuff*. It was one of the recipes I tried when the Cake Project began, and back then I pegged it as the penultimate pain-in-the-BEE-hind cake because it requires servitude—extra time in the kitchen to make mint syrup, a ganache, and chocolate fudge sauce.

But a funny thing happened between the first time I made Dark Chocolate Peppermint Pattie Cake and the last: I got better. Baking forty-plus cakes will do that to a gal. So while this cake is definitely trickier and more time-consuming than a basic Bundt, I don't consider it that difficult anymore. If you've been methodically working through these recipes in order, it should be no problem for you, either.

And it's not truly time-*consuming*; it's just one of those cakes where time *management* is needed. My best advice: pick a weekend day to make this cake. The night before, make the mint syrup and set it aside. The next morning, while having your coffee, make the ganache and set it aside. Go about your usual activities, stopping every so often in the kitchen to stir the ganache. About midafternoon return to the kitchen and make the cake. As soon as the cake goes in the oven, make the chocolate fudge sauce. Don't forget to stir the ganache in between.

By late afternoon, the cake should be cool enough to frost with the ganache.

Now, I can hear your question: "What's a ganache?" (That's ga-nosh.) It's a French word that translates literally as "jowl," and why they use it to describe a simple mixture of chocolate and dairy ingredients is beyond me. Maybe you develop jowls from eating ganache all the time. It's possible. A ganache is used as an icing or filling for any number of desserts and pastries, and quite Franc-ly, I prefer it over traditional, more sugary icings.

Dark Chocolate **Peppermint Pattie Cake** — CONTINUED

FOR THE CAKE

14 ounces semisweet or bittersweet chocolate
2 sticks (1 cup) unsalted butter
¼ cup plus 2 tablespoons heavy whipping cream
6 large eggs, separated
1 cup sugar
1 cup flour
½ teaspoon kosher salt
2 teaspoons vanilla extract
6 ounces small peppermint pattie candies

FOR THE CHOCOLATE FUDGE SAUCE (SEE TIP)

1 stick (½ cup) unsalted butter
½ cup brown sugar (light or dark)
⅓ cup sifted unsweetened cocoa
1 cup heavy whipping cream
Pinch of salt
½ teaspoon vanilla extract

FOR SERVING

Ice cream or sweetened whipped cream (homemade or in a can)

Tip: You can make the fudge sauce up to a week in advance and store in the refrigerator. You can also freeze it for future use.

TO MAKE THE MINT SYRUP (THE NIGHT *BEFORE* YOU MAKE YOUR CAKE)

1. Rinse your mint leaves and set aside.
2. In a small saucepan, combine the sugar and water. Bring to a boil over medium heat, then lower the heat and simmer for several minutes, until the sugar is completely dissolved. Remove from the heat and allow to cool completely.
3. Fill a small bowl with ice and water and put it near the stove.
4. Fill another saucepan about halfway with water and bring to a boil. Put the mint leaves in the water and blanch until they are just wilted, about 10 seconds. IMMEDIATELY strain the mint and plunge the leaves in that bowl of ice water. This sets the color. Strain the leaves one more time, then blot with paper towels.
5. In the food processor, combine the mint leaves and half the syrup. Puree the mint, stopping several times to scrape down the sides of the processor (puree is basically processing until nearly liquefied). Add the remaining syrup and puree for 2 more minutes.
6. Transfer the syrup to a clean storage container and allow to sit overnight, covered, at room temperature.

IN THE A.M.

7. Strain the syrup though a fine-mesh strainer and discard the solid parts. You can store the syrup in the refrigerator for up to 2 weeks. Make sure to shake before using.

CONTINUED —

Dark Chocolate **Peppermint Pattie Cake** – CONTINUED

TO MAKE THE GANACHE (ALSO IN THE A.M.)

8. In a food processor, finely chop your chocolate, baby.

9. Heat the cream in a heavy-bottomed saucepan to just under a boil.

   Add the chocolate, stirring constantly until the mixture is smooth. This will take about 10 to 15 minutes.

10. Remove from the heat. Pour the mixture through the medium strainer into a bowl and cool, stirring occasionally, until the mixture is thickened and spreadable.

NOW, you're not going to believe that the ganache is EVER going to be thick and spreadable, because when you first do this, the ganache looks like a dark chocolate oil slick. BUT, in about 5 hours, it's going to be the texture of putty, and that oil will be solidified into a white film. Do not panic. That's what fat does. Just stir everything back together again and move on with your mighty fine self.

TO MAKE THE CAKE

11. Center a rack and preheat the oven to 350 degrees F. Prepare the springform pan. Make sure to line the bottom with parchment paper AND spray the pan.

12. In a food processor, chop your chocolate coarsely, baby.

13. In the top of a double boiler over simmering water, melt the butter with the cream. Stir in the chocolate and continue stirring until the mixture is smooth. Remove from the heat and set aside.

14. In a mixer fitted with a whisk attachment, beat the egg yolks on medium-high speed, gradually adding the sugar, and continue beating until the mixture is light yellow and very thick. This will take about 5 minutes. Slow the mixer down, add the melted chocolate, and beat until just blended.

15. Dry whisk the flour and salt together in a separate bowl.

16. Replace the whisk attachment with the paddle or regular beaters. Add the flour to the mixture in thirds, beating after each addition until blended. Add the vanilla extract and beat until blended. The mixture will be thick. Remove from the mixer and set aside.

17. Dust the blade of a cleaver with flour and dice the peppermint patties on a lightly floured cutting board. You'll have to redust the blade as you go. You should have about 1 cup of diced patties. Set aside.

18. In a clean mixing bowl, with a clean, dry whisk attachment, beat the egg whites to medium-soft peaks. (Remember: soft peaks are between foamy and stiff peaks. When you remove the whisk from the egg whites, a soft peak will result, and will then gracefully slip back into the egg whites.)

19. Fold about a third of the egg whites into the chocolate mixture. Fold the remaining egg whites into the chocolate mixture, and finally, fold the peppermint patties into the batter.

20. Pour the batter into the prepared springform pan. Smooth the top with the back of a spoon or spatula.
21. Put the pan in the middle of the oven rack and bake for 45 to 50 minutes, until the cake tests done. The top of the cake will have cracks around the edges; don't fret. Nobody but you will know.
22. Cool the cake in the pan for 10 minutes. Remove the sides of the springform pan and cool the cake on a cake rack. When completely cooled, invert onto the serving plate and remove the parchment paper.

TO MAKE THE FUDGE SAUCE

23. On low heat, melt the butter in a medium saucepan.
24. Using a hand whisk, gently whisk in half of the brown sugar and cocoa. Add the remaining brown sugar and cocoa and whisk until incorporated.
25. Whisk in the cream and salt.
26. Bring the mixture to a simmer over medium-low heat, whisking often. Simmer for 8 to 10 minutes, until the sauce has thickened a bit.
27. Remove the sauce from the heat and whisk in the vanilla. Strain the sauce through a fine-mesh strainer.
28. Cool and serve at room temperature.

TO CONSTRUCT THE CAKE

Well, there's really not that much to tell.

29. Give your ganache a nice, strong stir until it's smooth. Cover the top (formerly the bottom) of your cake with the ganache, working it to the edges, but keeping if off the sides of the cake.
30. Serve with the fudge sauce, mint syrup, and ice cream or whipped cream.

WHAT? THERE'S *MORE* WORK?

Serving the cake is part of the servitude required of anyone making the Dark Chocolate Peppermint Pattie Cake. And it's one of the reasons it's the penultimate cake in this book and one of the reasons why, though it is fairly easy for me to make now, I still consider it somewhat of a pain-in-the-BEE-hind cake.

Upon slicing the cake, drizzle each slice with fudge sauce and mint syrup, and add a dollop of ice cream or a quick FFFFFT! of canned whipped cream.

When bringing this cake to the office, be sure to include a handy, dandy diagram for those who will serve themselves while you're busy actually getting some work done.

Stephen Pyles's Heaven and Hell Cake

THE LIBERACE OF LAYER CAKES

YOU'LL NEED

A heavy saucepan
2 to 3 medium bowls
Two 9-inch round cake pans
A whisk attachment and extra bowl for mixer

FOR THE GANACHE

2 cups heavy whipping cream
2 pounds milk chocolate, coarsely chopped, OR 2 pounds milk chocolate morsels

FOR THE ANGEL FOOD CAKE

2/3 cup cake flour
1 cup confectioners' sugar
1 cup egg whites (about 8 to 10 large egg whites)
Pinch of salt
1 teaspoon cream of tartar
2/3 cup sugar
1 teaspoon pure vanilla extract
1/2 teaspoon pure almond extract

FOR THE PEANUT BUTTER MOUSSE

12 ounces cream cheese, at room temperature
1 3/4 cups confectioners' sugar
2 cups creamy peanut butter, at room temperature
2 tablespoons heavy whipping cream

1 recipe Devil's Food Cake (page 173), but without the frosting and jam

CONTINUED —

Make this cake one time and they'll talk about it for years. It's CRA-zy! A layer of devil's food cake, covered with peanut butter-cream cheese mousse, followed by a layer of angel food, covered with more peanut butter-cream cheese mousse. The devil's food layer is repeated and topped with that last layer of angel food cake. The whole thing is covered in milk chocolate ganache and refrigerated for 2 hours before serving.

It is a tall cake. It is a rich cake. It teeters on the verge of being just too, too much cake. It flips people out. It is one outrageous cake.

It is also a cake that you cannot make correctly unless you've baked a whole lotta cake. Trust me. Been there, done that. Was better the second time around.

Now, who's Stephen Pyles? Chef Pyles is credited for revolutionizing Southwestern cuisine. He's a fifth-generation Texan, and the first Texan inducted into the James Beard Foundation's Who's Who of Food and Beverage in America. If you're ever in Dallas, you can go to his famous Star Canyon restaurant or his latest, the eponymous Stephen Pyles restaurant. Look for the Heaven and Hell Cake on the menus.

Yes, I know: ANOTHER Texas recipe! What is with Texans and their cakes?!

Chef Pyles told me he intended the name "Heaven and Hell" to refer to the angel food/devil's food combo, but he overheard a waitress one time telling customers "it's heaven on your lips and hell on your hips." He was a little annoyed with her at first until he realized it certainly wasn't hurting sales—Heaven and Hell Cake has long been his most popular desert. And many thanks to him for allowing me to share it with you.

A couple of caveats for this Fabulously Sweet Monstrosity: It does take a while to make and it may, indeed, be too much cake for you—I mean physically, too much cake. It is so tall, it does not fit in my cake carry. I have to remove the serving plate and put the cake flat on the bottom of the carry, which only leaves me with about a quarter of an inch of clearance when the lid is snapped on. Also, a mere slice of Heaven and Hell can easily be overwhelming for the palate and bloodstream of the average cake eater: too many flavors and too much chocolate at one time! And it can be a pain to slice: Angel food tends to be spongy, and the ganache gets thick after it has been in the fridge. A regular cake knife won't do: find a large serrated knife. Run it under hot water, and then slice through the cake. And forget about having a pristine first slice: that ain't gonna happen!

My best advice to you is this: Bake only 1 layer of devil's food cake and 1 layer of angel food on your first try. Just halve the ingredients for the cakes. Seriously. You can divide each layer, so you'll still end up with 4 layers of cake, but they'll be *thinner*, and you'll make the same amount of mousse and ganache. This will keep your co-workers from going into a sugar coma after one slice. It will also make the cake more physically manageable. Later, when you're serving hundreds daily (like Chef Pyles), or feeling particularly fabulous, put on your long sequined cape, your diamond dinner rings, break out your candelabrum, and go at it.

Stephen Pyles's ***Heaven and Hell Cake*** — CONTINUED

TO MAKE THE GANACHE (MAKE THIS EARLY)

1. Bring the cream to a boil over medium-high heat in a heavy saucepan. Remove from the heat, then gradually add the chocolate, whisking until smooth. Set aside to cool to room temperature.

I pour the hot mixture into a large metal bowl, rather than leave it in the hot saucepan. This helps dissipate the heat. I also stir several times while the ganache is cooling to room temperature. You're looking for it to get thick and spreadable. Because it's made with milk chocolate and not semisweet or bittersweet, this ganache will not be oily like the ganache for the Dark Chocolate Peppermint Pattie Cake (page 203).

TO MAKE THE ANGEL FOOD CAKE

2. Center a rack and preheat the oven to 375 degees F. Line two 9-inch cake pans with parchment paper. DO NOT SPRAY THE PANS.
3. Dry whisk the flour and confectioners' sugar together.
4. With the mixer on medium-low speed, beat the egg whites with the whisk attachment while adding the salt and cream of tartar. Increase the speed to medium-high and continue beating until soft peaks form. This will take about 1 minute.
5. Increase the mixer speed to medium and gradually add the regular (granulated) sugar, 1 tablespoon at a time, to the egg whites, beating until all the sugar is incorporated. Continuing beating for 1½ minutes more until stiff peaks form.
6. Reduce the mixer speed to low, add the vanilla extract and almond extract, and beat until just incorporated.
7. Remove the bowl from the mixer and sprinkle about half of the flour mixture over the top of the meringue. Fold the flour mixture into the egg whites, about 5 turns of the bowl. Repeat with the remaining flour. Do not overmix!
8. Gently spoon the batter into the prepared pans, mounding it slightly in the center.
9. Put the pans near the middle of the oven rack, without touching, and bake for 40 to 50 minutes, until the layers are golden brown and test done.
10. Cool the layers in the pan on a cake rack for 30 minutes, then unmold and and remove the parchment paper.

TO MAKE THE PEANUT BUTTER MOUSSE

11. With the mixer at medium speed, beat the softened cream cheese until it's light and creamy. While beating, gradually add the confectioners' sugar, and then the peanut butter. Add the heavy cream and continue beating until thoroughly blended. The mixture should be fluffy. Once finished, set aside.

TO MAKE THE DEVIL'S FOOD CAKE

12. Here's an economizing-your-time tip: If you only have 2 round cake pans, don't start making the batter until you've gotten the angel food layers out of the oven. By the time you're ready for a pan, the angel food will be cool and ready to unmold. Just be sure to clean your pans and prepare them before pouring the next cake.

TO CONSTRUCT THE CAKE

13. Now, the original directions call for dividing your layers, but because this cake is a lot of work and I find dividing angel cake in half particularly annoying, I've dispensed with that by having you bake 4 layers, total. Once the cakes are cooled, take your serrated knife or your Wilton cake cutter and even up the tops, if necessary.

14. Arrange 4 strips of wax paper in a square on the serving plate so that the edges of the bottom layer will sit on the paper. Remember to stack your layers *raw-crumb-side* down. Place a layer of devil's food cake on the wax paper. Spread a third of the peanut butter mousse on top.

15. Add a layer of angel food. Spread a third of the peanut butter mousse on top. Repeat with the second devil's food layer. Spread with the remaining mousse.

16. Crown the cake with the second angel food layer.

17. Whisk or stir the ganache one more time. Once it is thick enough to spread, go ahead and frost the top of your cake, then the sides. You should still have about a third of your ganache left. Put the cake in the refrigerator for 10 minutes to firm up the ganache, then bring it out and repeat, spreading with the remaining ganache.

18. Chill the cake in the refrigerator for at least 2 hours before serving. Serve it chilled. Don't forget to use that warm, wet knife to slice!

So, you've baked many a cake,

HUH?

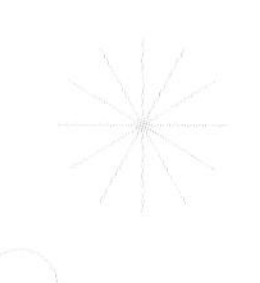

I HOPE YOU'RE FEELING PROUD OF YOURSELF AND READY TO TACKLE JUST ABOUT ANY CAKE RECIPE YOU COME ACROSS.

And now that you've baked fifty-plus cakes, I want you to pick up your favorite spatula in your left hand, hold it over your heart, raise your right hand in a victory sign, take a deep breath, and repeat after me:

"I hearby swear on Emma Rylander Lane's booze bottle, on Paula Deen's butter-coated ringed fingers, on Dorie Greenspan's easy buttercream frosting, on Mr. Dalquist's original Bundt pan, on Meemaw's dried apples, and on all the original cakes from the great state of Texas, that I will never, EVER, bake from a cake mix again."

Now go forth and collect your own recipes. Bake for your co-workers, your neighbors, your family, your friends. Keep notes and finesse as you see fit. Bring some homemade happiness into someone's harried, modern life, and be not cowed by flour, butter, eggs, and sugar ever again.

Thanks for indulging me. No go forth and indulge yourself.

Happy Baking!

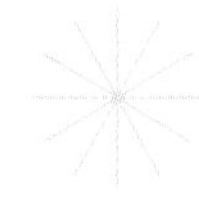

ACKNOWLEDGMENTS

This here book, as rambling and kooky as it is, would not have been possible without help and encouragement from the following people:

Susan Feeney, editor at *All Things Considered*, who, through simple repeated suggestion, pushed me to write this book. "This is Melissa. She bakes a cake every Monday. She's writing a book. It's called *All Cakes Considered*." Say it enough times, and I actually had to do it! She also got me in touch with Christy Fletcher, my literary agent. Thank you, Susan!

Michele Norris, one of the hosts of *All Things Considered*, who, because she so wanted to learn how to bake, decided to do a year's worth of occasional interviews with Dorie Greenspan, thus allowing me paid, professional time to learn even more about baking through working with Dorie.

Dorie Greenspan, baker extraordinaire and person extraordinaire, who cheered me, helped me problem solve, and otherwise worked her Evangelistic Baking Higher Power over me. Amen, sugar sister!

Ellen Silva, for all her proofreading, cake baking, cake eating, ego stroking, and constructive feedback.

My gal pals Julia Bailey, Dawn Benedetto, Kitty Eisele, and Marguerite Nutter for their encouragement and the occasional test baking.

The staff of *All Things Considered*, 2006 to the present: Jonathan "Smokey" Baer, Jesse Baker, Jonathan Blakely, Melissa Block, Brendan Banaszak, Julia Redpath Buckley, Neal Carruth, Franklyn Cater, Sonari Glinton, Jeremy Hobson, Andrea Hsu, Chelsea Jones, Carol Klinger, Viet Le, George Lyle, Alison Macadam, Raul Moreno, Quinn O'Toole, Bilal Qureshi, Rhonda Ray, Sara Sarasohn, Robert Siegel, Graham Smith, Elizabeth Tannen, Cory Turner, plus Krishnadev Calamur, Bill Deputy, Mary Glendenning, Robert Jackson, all of newscast, and some of *Morning Edition's* staff, most of whom gamely eat the cake every Monday and none of whom blame me for their expanding waistlines. Except Smokey. Smokey eats the cake, then blames me for his expanding waistline, and then for his depression on Tuesdays, when there is no cake. You guys remain a pleasure to bake for and an even greater pleasure to work with!

Special thanks to *All Things Considered* executive producer Christopher Turpin, who never, ever saw Monday cake as a negative distraction, and was (and still is) most enthusiastic and supportive of all my baking endeavors. Especially when they involve steamed puddings.

And last, but not least, my long-suffering spouse, Jimmy Argroves, who, lacking a sweet tooth, still tries slice after slice of whatever I'm making whenever I'm in doubt. The man deserves fried pie every day for the many times he's taken the cake out of the oven when I've had to go to bed, for the many times he's run out to the store when I've run out of butter, and for the many times he's done the dishes after a marathon day in the kitchen that wore me plain out. He's a good man, an excellent husband, and maybe the funniest guy I know. Maybe one day he'll like cake.

SOURCES

ONLINE SOURCES

Barker, Karen. "Dark Chocolate Peppermint Pattie Cake." The Food Network. *Sweet Dreams*. Episode: Southern Sweet Stuff. www.foodnetwork.com/food/cooking.

Block, Melissa. "Georgia Bill Puts Fried-Pie Lady Back in Business." *All Things Considered*, March 29, 2006. www.npr.org/templates/story/story.php?storyId=5310083.

Corriher, Shirley. "For Great Cakes, Get the Ratios Right." Taunton's Fine Cooking. www.taunton.com.

Deen, Paula. "Almond Sour Cream Pound Cake." The Food Network. *Paula's Home Cooking*. Episode: Paula Deen's Wedding. www.foodnetwork.com/food/cooking.

Deen, Paula. "Grandgirl's Fresh Apple Cake from Georgia." The Food Network. *Paula's Home Cooking*. Episode: Southern Seafood Show. www.foodnetwork.com/food/cooking.

Gray, Melissa. "The Cake Lady: Welcome at the Office." NPR.org, October 11, 2006. www.npr.org/templates/story/story.php?storyId = 6243629.

"Martha Washington's Great Cake." Mount Vernon: George Washington's Estate and Garden. www.mountvernon.org/learn/explore_mv/index.cfm/pid/289/.

Norris, Michele. "Cookbook Author Celebrates Apple Season." *All Things Considered*, October 19, 2007. www.npr.org/templates/story/story.php?storyId=15324538.

Norris, Michele. "Cookbook Author Explains Mysteries of Chocolate." *All Things Considered*, February 13, 2007. www.npr.org/templates/story/story.php?storyId=7329088.

"Summer Food: Mother Knows Best." *All Things Considered*, August 15, 2007. www.npr.org/templates/story/story.php?storyId=12809371.

USEFUL WEB SITES

About.com: Home Cooking, www.homecooking.about.com, includes "Cinnamon History, " by Peggy Trowbridge Filippone.

Ask Uncle Phaedrus, www.hungrybrowser.com, is a recipe question-and-answer site.

The Cook's Thesaurus, www.foodsubs.com, is a cooking encylopedia.

The Food Timeline, www.foodtimeline.org, includes information on the history of cake.

Joy of Baking.com, www.joyofbaking.com, is a recipe and food history site.

Kitchen Project, www.kitchenproject.com, is another recipe and food history site.

Leite's Culinaria, www.leitesculinaria.com, is, yup, a recipe and food history site.

McCormick, www.mccormick.com, is the spice company's Web site.

Nordic Ware, www.nordicware.com, is the bakeware company's Web site.

Pillsbury, www.pillsbury.com, is also a company Web site.

Washington Apples, www.bestapples.com, is the Washington Apple Commission's Web site.

NEWSPAPERS

Birr, Sara. "Angel Food Cake Recipes." *Newhouse News Service*: September 13, 2007

Bruno, Debra. "The Cake through Which I Came to Know My Grandmother." *The Washington Post*. May 17, 2007

Chang, Kenneth. "Flour, Eggs, Sugar, Chocolate... Just Add Chemistry." *The New York Times*, December 28, 2004.

Fabricant, Florence. "So Naughty, So Nice." *The New York Times*, February 14, 2007.

Ford, Meredith. "Red Velvet Valentine." *The Atlanta Journal Constitution*, February 14, 2008,

Kaufman, Sheila. "Tradition: Apples and Honey." *The Washington Post*, September 13, 2006, Food Section.

Lambert, Leigh. "The Tale of One Cool Cookie." *The Washington Post*, June 13, 2007.

Stuever, Hank. "The Bundt Pan Man, Letting Them Eat Cake." *The Washington Post*, January 11, 2005.

BOOKS

Berolzheimer, Ruth, ed. *The American Woman's Cook Book*. New York: Garden City Publishing, 1943.

Better Homes and Gardens New Cook Book. Des Moines: Bantam Books, 1953 and 1971.

Cora, Cat. *Cooking from the Hip*. New York: Houghton Mifflin, 2007.

Culinary Arts Institute, *200 Classic Cake Recipes*. Chicago, Ill.: Consolidated Book Publishers, 1969.

Eckhardt, Linda West. *Cakes from Scratch in Half the Time*. San Francisco: Chronicle Books, 2005.

Greenspan, Dorie. *Baking: From My Home to Yours*. New York: Houghton Mifflin, 2006.

Lagasse, Emeril. *Emeril's Potluck*. New York: HarperCollins, 2004.

Lee, Harper. *To Kill a Mockingbird*. New York: Harper Perennial Modern Classics, 2005.

Lukins, Sheila. *U.S.A. Cookbook*. New York: Workman, 1997.

McDermott, Nancie. *Southern Cakes: Sweet and Irresistible Recipes for Everyday Celebrations*. San Francisco: Chronicle Books, 2007.

Nenes, Michael F. *American Regional Cuisine,* 2nd ed. Hoboken, N.J.: John Wiley & Sons, 2007.

Providence Baptist Church. *Sharing Our Best: Providence Baptist Church Homecoming Edition*. Collierville, Tenn.: Fundcraft, 2000.

Southern Living 2005 Annual Recipes. Birmingham, AL: Oxmoor House, 2006.

Walter, Carole. *Great Cakes*. New York: Clarkson Potter, 1991.

Wister, Owen. *Lady Baltimore*. Chicago: J.S. Sanders, 1992.

INDEX

D

E

F

G

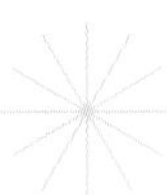

Table of EQUIVALENTS

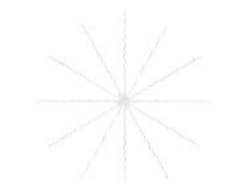

The exact equivalents in the following tables have been rounded for convenience.

LIQUID/DRY MEASUREMENTS

U.S.	METRIC
¼ teaspoon	1.25 milliliters
½ teaspoon	2.5 milliliters
1 teaspoon	5 milliliters
1 tablespoon (3 teaspoons)	15 milliliters
1 fluid ounce (2 tablespoons)	30 milliliters
¼ cup	60 milliliters
⅓ cup	80 milliliters
½ cup	120 milliliters
1 cup	240 milliliters
1 pint (2 cups)	480 milliliters
1 quart (4 cups; 32 ounces)	960 milliliters
1 gallon (4 quarts)	3.84 liters
1 ounce (by weight)	28 grams
1 pound	448 grams
2.2 pounds	1 kilogram

OVEN TEMPERATURES

FAHRENHEIT	CELSIUS	GAS
250	120	½
275	140	1
300	150	2
325	160	3
350	180	4
375	190	5
400	200	6
425	220	7
450	230	8
475	240	9
500	260	10

LENGTHS

U.S.	METRIC
⅛ inch	3 millimeters
¼ inch	6 millimeters
½ inch	12 millimeters
1 inch	2.5 centimeters